GROWING PAINS

Gwynne Dyer has worked as a freelance journalist, columnist, author, broadcaster, and lecturer on international affairs for more than twenty years. His twice-weekly column on international affairs is published by 175 newspapers in some forty-five countries and is translated into more than a dozen languages. He is the author of several books, including *War*, *Future: Tense*, *The Mess They Made*, and *Climate Wars*.

To Susan and Dennis, Mary and Keith, Dave and Rhonda, Jeff and Eleanor, and Reinhold and Lissa — and their kids, of course. I am fortunate in my brothers and sisters, and just as much in my brothers- and sisters-in-law.

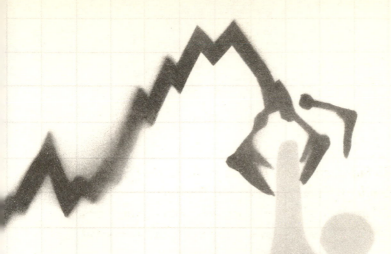

GROWING PAINS

The future of
democracy
(and work)

GWYNNE DYER

SCRIBE
Melbourne • London

Scribe Publications
18–20 Edward St, Brunswick, Victoria 3056, Australia
2 John Street, Clerkenwell, London, WC1N 2ES, United Kingdom

First published by Scribe 2018

Printed and bound in the UK by CPI Group (UK) Ltd,
Croydon, CR0 4YY.

Scribe Publications is committed to the sustainable use of natural
resources and the use of paper products made responsibly from
those resources.

9781925322637 (Australian edition)
9781911344759 (UK edition)
9781947534070 (US edition)
9781925548433 (e-book)

A CiP entry for this title is available from the National Library of
Australia and the British Library.

scribepublications.com.au
scribepublications.co.uk
scribepublications.com

Contents

1

A giant orange canary

This is not a book about Donald Trump. It is an inquiry into the new political reality that has been revealed by his election and the events that have accompanied it. We thought we had enough on our plate already: war and global warming, tribalism and terrorism, artificial intelligence and the Sixth Mass Extinction. Suddenly it turns out that we will have to cope with all these problems and challenges, some of them very frightening indeed, while simultaneously dealing with a huge shift in our basic social, economic, and political relationships.

We owe Donald Trump a vote of thanks, because he has inadvertently done us a great service. He is the canary in the coalmine — a giant orange canary — and he has made us aware of a growing threat to democratic societies that we should have noticed but didn't. He didn't do it by toppling off his perch, dead, poisoned by the accumulation of explosive gases, as the traditional small yellow canaries did. He did it simply by getting elected to the presidency of the United States, an outcome so unexpected and implausible that people realised right away that something had gone seriously wrong.

Trump's election has created two different sets of anxieties in the rest of the world (and in many Americans, too, of course). The first is simply that Trump's ignorance, his vanity, and his impulsiveness make a major war more likely than it has been at any time since the late 1980s. This is a quite understandable fear, because even in this remarkably peaceful era there are still 'flash-points' such as the Korean peninsula and the Middle East where a relatively short series of bad decisions could draw the great powers into proxy wars, or even into direct clashes. But that probably is not going to happen.

Low-probability events do occasionally come to pass, but it's hard to believe that even North Korea's nuclear and ballistic missile tests will lead to a great-power war in northeast Asia. The grown-ups are still in charge in China, in Japan, in Russia, and in South Korea, and they really don't want such a war. If Donald Trump and his North Korean adversary, Kim Jong-un, seem a trifle unhinged from time to time, that is cause for concern, but not really for panic.

The Middle East is more worrisome, because both Russian and American troops are already on the ground in different parts of Syria, and two of the most powerful leaders in the region, Saudi Arabia's crown prince, Mohammed bin Salman, and Turkey's president, Recep Tayyip Erdoğan, are as belligerent and as erratic as Donald Trump. But even direct US-Russian clashes in Syria would almost certainly not lead to a nuclear war: the military establishments in both countries, and President Vladimir Putin himself, have absolutely no desire to go down that road.

I'll go into these questions further in Chapter Two, but let us assume for the moment that a major war that involves great powers on both sides is very unlikely in the next few years. The real worries have more to do with the long-term integrity of the system, for many people saw a pattern in Trump's rise that reminded them of the last time populism and ultra-nationalism overwhelmed democratic politics and the rule of law in some Western democracies. This is not to say that Donald Trump is a fascist — that would require more abstract thinking and self-discipline than he seems capable of — but, despite all his tweets and other 21st-century political techniques, there is a strong whiff of the 1930s about him.

In the months following Trump's election there was something approaching panic in European political circles. The local neo-fascists and simple racists seemed to have the wind in their sails, and the 'domino theory' was resurrected from its shallow grave. In this scenario, the United States played the role of first domino to fall (although some argued that pro-Brexit Britain had really led the way six months previously), and the elections in the Netherlands, France, and even Germany were going to go the same way in the course of 2017.

Well, they didn't, and the immediate panic is past. Now European opinion has swung to the other extreme, and has re-defined the problem as a purely American phenomenon, or at most an aberration of the 'Anglosphere'. That is not true either.

In the Dutch parliamentary election of March 2017, Geert Wilders, the most notorious source of nativist, authoritarian, populist, and rabidly anti-Muslim rhetoric in the Netherlands, won only five extra seats in parliament — but his party is now the second-largest of the thirteen parties in the Dutch House of Representatives.

In the French presidential elections of 2002, Jean-Marie Le Pen, the openly anti-Semitic, anti-immigrant, neo-fascist founder of the National Front, managed to squeak into the second round because the anti-fascist vote had been split between so many other parties in the first round. However, he then got only 17 per cent of the vote when faced with a single rival in the run-off. Whereas in last year's presidential election his daughter Marine Le Pen, who inherited the party leadership and most of his ideas (although she is a far smoother operator), also made it into the second round of voting — and then doubled her father's share of the vote in the run-off to 34 per cent. One-third of the French men and women who voted in the second round this time gave their votes to a neo-fascist.

And in the German elections of September 2017, the two 'mainstream' parties together got barely half the vote, while one German in eight voted for the radical-right Alternativ für Deutschland, which shades off into neo-Nazism on its far right.

So the phenomenon that produced Trump, whatever

it may be, also exists in Europe, but it seems to be less advanced there. The explanation for this striking difference between American and European politics, after a decade of low economic growth on both sides of the Atlantic, probably lies in the far greater inequality of incomes in the United States. On the assumption that it is the size of the gap between the rich and the poor, rather than the absolute level of incomes, that causes the greatest political resentment, one would expect the United States to have the biggest problem: the top 20 per cent of Americans earn about eight times what the bottom 20 per cent get. The United Kingdom, as one would expect, is the EU member whose politics most closely resemble those of the US, as the top fifth of British earners are paid seven times as much as the bottom fifth, and there too the radical nationalists are in power. They are not in power, or at least not yet, in the Netherlands, France, or Germany, where the income gap between the top fifth and the bottom fifth is just over five times greater.

The fact that the European welfare states are more comprehensive and more generous than that of the United States may also be relevant, but income disparities alone may be enough to account for the higher levels of envy, resentment, and anger, and the political consequences of all those negative emotions, in the United States.

Cast the net even wider, and the results are still the same. Canada closely resembles the United States in most respects, and Canadian and American average incomes are virtually identical, but Canada's politics are far less combative and extreme. Why? Probably because the disparity between the incomes of the top 20 per cent of Canadians and the bottom 20 per cent is the same as it is in France (5.5 times) and quite unlike the United States (8 times). And Japan, whose politics are a byword for stability, has the lowest income disparity of any developed country. Correlation does not necessarily mean causation, but it's a pretty safe bet that there is a connection here, and I will be returning to this subject.

So then: is it all a mirage? Is there no populist wave, just the United States having a hard time (or at least a bizarre one), and everybody else muddling through as usual? Or is it at least only a case of the 'Anglosphere' vs. the rest? (England has gone off the rails, too.) And can it really all be so easily explained just by income disparities? If, when Pat Moynihan persuaded president Richard Nixon to send a proposal to Congress for a Family Assistance Program (a guaranteed income for the poor) in 1969, that bill had made it through Congress, the disparity of income between rich Americans and the rest would suddenly have narrowed to European or Canadian levels. And in that case, would the president of the United States today resemble Justin Trudeau more than Donald Trump?

Obviously not. A country is more than just its economic arrangements. It has deeply embedded traditions and habits and even ideals, and they are subtly or hugely different, depending on which countries you are comparing. You can't reduce it all to a simple formula. So the answer to the larger question — was it all a mirage? — is no, it wasn't, but you can't reduce it to a lockstep or a row of dominoes either. It does seem like the United States is going through some sort of reckoning for past mistakes, and that it will emerge from the process changed in various ways, for better or for worse. The same is largely true for England, but it doesn't yet feel that such a profound change is underway in most European countries. Yet it may come to that in the end. The West is one civilisation — which includes Russia, no matter what the Slavophiles think — in many local varieties. Economic trends, political styles, and ideological fashions do spread right across it in a short number of years.

As for the notion that 'populism' in the Trump style is spreading beyond the confines of the West and changing the wider world beyond, that is far from self-evident. Rodrigo Duterte in the Philippines, the soldiers now running Thailand, and Egypt's General al-Sisi are just standard-issue thugs in politics; the only new thing about them is that they are recent arrivals in power. These countries, and dozens more like them, are reinventing democracy for themselves — you can't export it — and there is bound to be a lot of back-and-forth in the early years. The first eighty years after the Revolution in France were also pretty turbulent, and roughly the same length of time after the American Revolution the country was being consumed by a great civil war. Democratic politics is hard, no doubt about it, and there are practically bound to be setbacks.

Across the 'West', however, there is enough common ground that the same factors may well be fuelling the rise of populism on both sides of the Atlantic. This is a matter of great concern, even if we are not heading for a future of storm troopers and death camps. As the bill comes due for the two-century boom in human population and consumption triggered by the Industrial Revolution, we are moving into a future that will be a lot more difficult and dangerous than the present or the recent past. Climate change, mass migration, ocean acidification, global food shortages: we will face multiple converging crises at the same time, and the last thing we need in charge of dealing with them is simple-minded, short-sighted, and incompetent populist governments.

The potential for disaster would still be high even if we were all ruled by Plato's philosopher-kings. In real life, the best we can hope for is democratic governments led by intelligent and honest politicians who respect the rule of law. Not all countries that call themselves democratic have that even now, but if the trend that became evident in 2016 prospers and spreads, our governments will be totally incapable of dealing with these crises by the time they actually hit us in five, ten, or fifteen years from now.

> Governments with resources will be forced to engage in long, nightmarish episodes of triage, deciding who and what can be salvaged from engulfment by a disordered environment. The choices will need to be made primarily among the poorest, not just abroad but at home. We have already previewed the images, in the course of the organisational and spiritual unravelling that was Hurricane Katrina. At progressively more

extreme levels, the decisions will be increasingly harsh: morally agonising to those who must make them — but in the end morally deadening.

Professor Leon Fuerth, member of the Principals' Committee of the National Security Council, 1993–2000

Such tragedies may already be inevitable, but they may also still be contingent on the decisions that governments take in the present and the near future. It's therefore still worth proceeding on the assumption that global catastrophe is not inevitable, and that what governments do matters a lot. For that reason, if for no other, we need to understand why crude populists are doing better in elections even in long-established democracies, and how far the rot is likely to spread.

What is the secret elixir that populists such as Trump have stumbled upon that is enabling them to overthrow the existing political rules and win power? Best to ask them, or just listen to what they say in public. Trump's own explanation for his success is quite simple: immigrants (too many of them) and jobs (too few of them).

Trump frequently links these two themes, claiming that the immigrants are stealing the jobs of (white, native-born) American workers, but that doesn't really hold water. The key 'Rust Belt' states where the votes of working-class whites (many of them former Democratic voters) gave Trump the victories that made him president were Pennsylvania, Michigan, and Wisconsin.

These three states are home to only 1.7 million foreign-born residents out of a total population of 28.5 million, or just under 6 per cent of the whole.[1] The proportion of immigrants in the US population as a whole is more than twice that: 14.3 per cent. Immigrants don't go to the Rust Belt states in significant numbers, because there are very few jobs to be had there.

Many former Democratic voters in these predominantly white states voted for Donald Trump, but it certainly wasn't because they had lost their jobs to immigrants. However, they really had lost their jobs, or at best had lost their old, well-paying jobs and were now working for the minimum wage. They were looking for the reason why, and the other explanation Trump offered them was that their jobs had been stolen by other countries. The cars that used to be made in Detroit are now built in central Mexico, and the steel that was once made in Pennsylvania is now produced in Hebei province in China.

Trump's promise to 'bring the jobs home' was probably the key factor in getting him elected, but the truth is that most of the jobs had never left the United States. About 5.6m manufacturing jobs were lost in the United States between 2000 and 2010, but a study by the Center for Business and Economic Research at Ball State University concluded that 85 per cent of those jobs were eliminated by technological change. In most cases, they were automated out of existence.[2]

The real culprits were not the immigrants or the foreigners; they were the computers and the robots. But you are not going to get very far in an election campaign if you blame the machines. There's nothing a politician can plausibly promise to do that would stop automation, so the safer course is not to mention it at all — and neither Donald Trump nor Hillary Clinton did. Instead, both politicians peddled a sepia-tinted fantasy of crowded assembly lines and the return of the Good Old Days: Clinton's platform implausibly promised 'a full-employment economy where everyone has a job that pays enough to raise a family and live in dignity'. However, Trump left Clinton in the dust by blaming the job losses on people — foreigners — whom he was going to blackmail or bully into giving the jobs back. He may even believe that himself: he's a developer, and he knows little or nothing about the world of manufacturing.

The rise of automation is not exactly a new topic. Experts have been predicting that mechanisation, and later automation, will eliminate huge numbers of jobs for at least fifty years now. But the job apocalypse was very slow to arrive, and eventually most people just filed that prediction under 'false prophecies'. Even now, people will argue that the lost manufacturing jobs are being replaced by equal or larger numbers of service jobs that pay just as well. However, the number of new jobs being created is really far inferior to the number being destroyed; they are not necessarily in the same places, which is why the big Rust Belt cities feel half-abandoned; and as the algorithms get smarter, the service jobs are starting to go, too.

And there is a further, underlying culprit that was never directly addressed by Hillary Clinton (although Bernie Sanders talked about it quite a lot, and Trump at least knew what the problem was, although he misdiagnosed the cause). American middle-class incomes have stagnated for several decades, and working-class incomes have actually declined somewhat, for reasons that have only a tenuous connection to globalisation and little if anything to do with automation. 'Neo-liberalism', the dominant and one could almost say exclusive economic doctrine of the past thirty-five years, has involved an unstated but quite direct attack on the incomes of hourly-paid Americans, and many salaried ones as well.

As an example of what this means, in only one of the largest twenty-five metropolitan areas in the United States (Washington, D.C.) can a household on the median local income afford the average price of a new car.[3] This is not a limitless disaster — most households can still afford a used car of some sort — but it does mean that people who always used to be able to buy a new one are feeling hard done by. They are working as hard as ever, but for some invisible reason they are falling behind. Many of them will grasp at any plausible reason they are offered, even if it isn't the true one. But this question of what has happened to the incomes of those who still have work in America is a large topic, and is dealt with at greater length in Chapter Five.

The Giant Canary's election certainly focused people's attention on the large number of Americans who are unemployed, underpaid, or living in fear of unemployment, because it was their votes that put Trump in office. (Most of the people who voted for him, of course, were just habitual Republican voters who felt they had no other option but to support their party's candidate, but there were not enough of them to put Trump in the White House without those extra votes from the white working-class voters, especially in the Rust Belt.) There was a post-election feeding frenzy as the American media investigated this curious new political phenomenon that they had not previously noticed under their noses, so now unemployment, de-industrialisation, automation, and even the shifting distribution of incomes in America (take from the poor, give to the rich) are hot topics. But most commentators and analysts have still not grasped the true nature and scale of the challenge, because they have no idea what the real unemployment rate in the United States is.

> Don't believe those phony numbers when you hear 4.9 and 5 per cent unemployment. The number's probably 28, 29, as high as 35. In fact, I even heard recently 42 per cent.
>
> Donald Trump's victory speech after the New Hampshire primary, 10 February 2016

At the time of writing, the official US unemployment rate is 4.5 per cent, but that only counts those men and women who are actively looking for a job. It does *not* count the considerably larger number of Americans of working age, physically and mentally able to work, who have simply stopped looking for a job. There may be none available in their area, or at least none that pay well enough to justify abandoning the unemployment benefits, welfare payments, or other small sources of income that they depend on, but they have essentially given up. If you include all those who are not working and not just the job-seekers, 17.5 per cent of American men of prime working age (24–55) are, in the true sense of the word, 'unemployed'.[4] That is one in six. The last time US unemployment was at this level was in 1936, halfway through the Great Depression.

But if this is true, how could we have missed it? During the Great Depression there were massive strikes and hunger marches, and dozens of workers were shot dead by the police or the National Guard; now the only evidence of the anger of the unemployed is their votes. The difference is almost certainly due to the welfare states that were created in every Western democracy after the Second World War, at least partly in order to avoid the kind of extreme misery and anger on the part of the unemployed that paved the way to fascism and war in the 1930s. Even in the United States, whose welfare state is rudimentary, it has served to take the edge off popular anger.

The unemployed aren't actually trying to hide, but they have many ways of vanishing from the statistics. For example, a great many unemployed Americans have managed to wangle their way onto disability benefits. Between 2000 and 2013, the number of American workers receiving payments under the Social Security Disability Insurance programme almost doubled, from 5 million to almost 9 million — and between 1982 and 2013, the proportion of disability payments awarded for hard-to-disprove conditions such as mental illness and back pain rose from 27 per cent to 53 per cent.[5] This is not to say that most Americans claiming disabilities are not really disabled, of course, but any system can be gamed, and given the very large number of people receiving unemployment or welfare payments, it is not surprising that some would choose the rather less onerous alternative of disability payments.

This submerged reef of unemployed people is biggest south of the Great Lakes in the Rust Belt, the former industrial heartland of the United States, where automation has been extremely efficient in destroying manufacturing jobs. It would be a mistake to assume that the victims of this process, since they are not actually seeking work, must be disengaged and apathetic about their fate. They are normal human beings, so a large proportion of them feel humiliated, abandoned by their fellow-countrymen, and very angry. Indeed, a critical number of former Democratic voters in the Rust Belt were so angry that they switched to Trump and put him into the White House.

The situation is not quite the same in the United Kingdom, where hostility to immigration and downright racism, especially in non-metropolitan areas, played an even bigger role in the pro-Brexit vote than it did in the pro-Trump vote, and unemployment got much less attention. This was partly because the leading Brexiteers, most of whom were members of the governing Conservative Party, had no incentive to attack their own party's record on employment, but it also helped that the unemployment rate was considerably lower than in the United States and that the British welfare state was rather more generous.

However, the official British unemployment figure of 4.8 per cent is almost as fictional as its American equivalent, the true number probably being close to twice that. A report by Sheffield Hallam University's Centre for Regional Economic and Social Research reckons that almost one-third of the people on incapacity benefits in Britain would be working in a full-employment economy, and that the true jobless rate in some northern post-industrial areas reaches 17 per cent.[6] As many as two-thirds of the local population voted 'Leave' in some of these areas, and in age, circumstances, and attitudes they closely resembled the 'angry white men' (and women) who were the key group that pushed Trump over the threshold of the White House in the US election. The same observations apply in large measure to the last French and German elections.

In every case, the anger translated into a resurgence of nationalism in its various mutually exclusive national forms, and in every case except Germany it also fed on a strong suspicion among the working class and much of the middle class that the very rich had mutated into a new species that was leaving them ever further behind. And since a large section of the media is owned and controlled by members of that new species, the anger is systematically redirected against minorities and foreigners in order to protect their interests.

I should add that the media herd in the United States has recently moved away from economic explanations for the Trump victory, possibly feeling that they overdid the visits to heartland diners and sympathy for the forgotten white working class that filled their stories for much of the past year. Or maybe that explanation was just getting old, and they needed a new story-line. At any rate, now it's more about the innate racism and social conservatism of the white working class. There's no question that Trump has exploited that with ruthless efficiency, but this new approach confuses cause and effect.

Of course the white working class are socially conservative, and many of them are racists. They always were, and Republicans have been exploiting that for several decades. But why are they now so radicalised: more racist, more nationalist, more ready to vote for a crude populist like Trump? It is because they are more desperate, and they are desperate because the economy has cast them aside.

> According to our estimates around 47 per cent of total US employment is in the high risk category. We refer to these as jobs at risk — *i.e.* jobs we expect could be automated relatively soon, perhaps over the next decade or two.
>
> Carl Benedikt Frey and Michael A. Osborne, *The Future of Employment: how susceptible are jobs to computerisation?* Oxford Martin School, 17 September 2013

Only American workers have been told (by Trump) that their jobs were stolen by foreigners, but the truth is that they are going everywhere, and that both in the United States and elsewhere they are actually being destroyed mostly by automation. The Oxford Martin School study was the first of many. An OECD working paper in 2016 referred to studies suggesting that roughly 42 per cent of jobs in Germany, 35 per cent in the United Kingdom, 33 per cent in Canada, and 30 per cent in France, Sweden, and Japan are highly susceptible to automation.[7] In the same year, a Citibank study estimated that 57 per cent of jobs were at risk across the European Union as a whole, while 69 per cent of Indian and 77 per cent of Chinese *manufacturing* jobs (non-manufacturing jobs were not considered in these cases) could also be easily replaced by automation.[8] A more recent study released in March 2017 by financial services firm PwC (PricewaterhouseCoopers) revisited the United States, and predicted 38 per cent job losses to automation in the next fifteen years.[9]

Now, you can argue that not all the jobs that can be replaced by automation will be replaced, and you would certainly be right in some cases: it will continue to be cheaper to use human workers, or the jobs will be protected by legislation and regulation, or the customers will simply want to deal with people and not machines. You can question the research methodology and/or the mathematics. But you cannot deny that this is huge change, and coming fast. In fact, it will probably turn out to be social and economic change on a scale comparable to the Industrial Revolution, when England went from being a largely agrarian country, with only 34 per cent of its population living in cities and towns in 1801, to an industrialised country with 78 per cent of its people living in urban areas by 1901. This time, however, it's happening at least twice as fast, and all over the world at about the same time. For example, while Indian manufacturing production is growing very fast and will continue to do so, automation is spreading fast, too, and there is a serious public debate in India about whether *employment* in manufacturing may be peaking right now.

Disruptive as the Industrial Revolution was, industrialisation just moved people from one kind of employment to another. The change this time is moving people out of employment permanently. Historically, mass unemployment brings political radicalisation with it, and there is no reason to believe that things will work differently this time.

We're not going to stop the automation, so the problem is going to grow steadily bigger. To avoid a social and political catastrophe, we will have to find ways of putting real money into the pockets of those who have no work. Moreover, we will have to find ways of subsidising people without humiliating them and treating them like 'losers', because that's what really drove the anger that put Trump in office. Otherwise, the populist demagogues who get elected in twenty years' time may make us look back fondly on the Trump years.

If automation is really undermining the social contract that democratic systems depend on, the highest priority is to rewrite that contract in terms that ensure that those who are most affected by the shift away from a full-employment society are not punished economically or isolated socially. As it happens, ideas about how to do that soon began to tumble out into the mainstream media.

Within a couple of months there was a widely shared working hypothesis about what had led to the election of a man like Trump: it was the grievances of the unemployed, the underpaid, and the about-to-be-unemployed. Not everybody was clear on the connection between automation and mass unemployment, or on how the sheer numbers of the unemployed were hidden by the official statistics. The extent to which the incomes of more than two-thirds of the population had stagnated or even fallen since the turn of the century in almost all the developed countries was old news to the experts, but it came as a revelation to many ordinary people. Nevertheless, there was soon a common understanding that the job famine and low incomes were radicalising large numbers of people who had previously accepted the status quo, and that their anger was being exploited by ruthless populists. By early 2017, there was already a proposal on the table for heading off the most frightening consequences of that anger. It is called Universal Basic Income (UBI).

UBI is now a hot topic in political circles and in the media throughout the developed democratic countries, because it is seen as a possible way of taking the political curse off mass unemployment (a phrase that will eventually be replaced by some gentler euphemism in order to make it respectable). Nobody knows whether it is really affordable to give every adult in rich post-industrial societies an unconditional basic income adequate to sustain a modest but comfortable life style regardless of whether they are employed or not. But it might be possible — and that is certainly what is being suggested.

The political attractiveness of a UBI lies in the fact that if every citizen is getting the benefit in question (as in the case of state-sponsored old age pensions), there is no humiliation in receiving it. Everybody has enough money to get by, nobody gets singled out as a failure because they don't have a job, and therefore nobody (or at least not a large number of voters) drifts into the state of resentment and incoherent rage that did so much to facilitate the election of Donald Trump. That, at any rate, is the theory.

> For centuries this has been considered a utopia, but today it has not only become possible, but indispensable.
>
> Ralph Kundig, campaigner for Basic Income Switzerland, Agence France-Presse, 5 June 2016

> Theoretically, if Switzerland were an island, the answer is yes. But with open borders, it's a total impossibility, especially for Switzerland, with a high living standard. If you would offer every individual a Swiss amount of money, you would have billions of people who would try to move into Switzerland.
>
> Luzi Stamm, member of parliament for the right-wing Swiss Peoples' Party, BBC, 5 June 2016

UBI may be a seductive idea for policy wonks, but it is definitely not ready yet for prime time with the voters.

In June 2016, Switzerland held a referendum on a universal basic income that would have given each adult Swiss citizen 2,500 Swiss francs ($US 2,600) per month, and each child SFR 625 ($650). This is not as lavish as it sounds, given the very high cost of living in Switzerland — in terms of purchasing-power parity, it would be more like $US 1,500 per adult and $400 per child — but it is unquestionably a serious amount of money.

In Switzerland (as in California), you only have to collect enough signatures to get a proposal on the ballot papers (100,000 signatures within eighteen months, in the Swiss case), and when the referendum rolled around the activists who sponsored the UBI proposal pulled no punches. They advocated a truly universal basic income that would have gone to every Swiss citizen over the age of eighteen, whether they were working or not. The referendum's sponsors even estimated the total cost to the federal budget: an additional 25 billion Swiss francs per year (around 5 per cent of GDP). It was the first-ever political test of a revolutionary idea that few people had even heard of until recently — so the horrified Swiss rejected it by a majority of more than three to one. Of course. The sponsors weren't even surprised.

But 23 per cent of Swiss voters said yes to the idea, and even right-wing politicians such as Luzi Stamm were not necessarily opposed in principle. ('Theoretically … the answer is yes'). Stamm was only put off by the fear of millions of foreign freeloaders (who in real life would be stopped at the borders, and even if they did get in could not access the UBI payments because they would not be Swiss citizens). As Ralph Kundig of BIEN (Basic

Income Earth Network) said, 'Just getting a broad public debate started on this important issue is a victory.'

At about the same time, an opinion poll conducted by Dalia Research among 10,000 people in all twenty-eight EU countries found that 64 per cent would vote in favour of a UBI, while only 24 per cent would vote against it. (Twelve per cent would not vote.) They were probably less well informed about UBI than the Swiss voters, but the question clearly stated that UBI was 'an income unconditionally paid by the government to every individual regardless of whether they work and irrespective of any other sources of income. It replaces other social security payments and is high enough to cover all basic needs (food, housing, etc.).'

The poll also asked people what would the impact of UBI be on their work choices. Thirty-four per cent said it would have no effect, 15 per cent said they would reduce their working hours and spend more time with their families, 10 per cent said they would take time off to gain additional skills, 7 per cent said they would look for a different job, 5 per cent said they would work as a freelancer — and only 4 per cent said they would stop working.[10]

The Swiss referendum and the Dalia poll both took place before the Great Trump Shock; but only six months later, with President Trump in office and the sources of his victory clear, half-a-dozen governments were launching pilot programmes to road-test the idea of a basic income. Finland's is a timid little thing that gives the participants in the trial just $600 per month, and it certainly isn't universal. It only goes to jobless people who are receiving the lowest level of unemployment benefit. But the Canadian one is much more robust.

In April 2016, the province of Ontario launched a pilot programme that pays out much more than the Finns — CAD $1,400 a month (US $1,050) for a single individual — and you don't have to be unemployed to get it, just poor. 'The project will explore the effectiveness of providing a basic income to people who are currently living on low incomes, whether they are working or not,' explained Ontario Premier Kathleen Wynne. But the payments are still going only to poor people, so the recipients are still stigmatised — and the supporters of the Ontario programme are keen to stress that the ultimate goal is to get people back into work. As in Finland, they believe (or at least profess to believe) that the only real solution to poverty is full employment.

In the early 21st century, this quaint belief is about as credible as the Easter Bunny, and it is doubtful that the people behind these pilot projects believe it themselves. One suspects that if they had their wish, they would be testing the viability of a really universal basic income — everybody gets it, rich or poor, employed or not — but they think the outcry against that would be too great. Like the other pilot programmes in Italy, the Netherlands, and Scotland, what they are really testing at the moment are various streamlined versions of traditional unemployment and welfare payments for the jobless, and income-support programmes for the working poor, with one major exception: in these programmes, the guaranteed basic income does not shrink or stop if the recipient has another source of income, like a job. But the data they draw from these tests (which will run from three to five years) will answer some of the key questions surrounding the concept, such as whether people in receipt of UBI are really likely to stay in their jobs, or (in the case of the unemployed) take on a new job if there is one available.

There are no plans to introduce a full UBI at the moment, and even if the results drawn from the current pilot programmes are positive, it is highly unlikely that we will see UBI operating anywhere at a national scale in the next five years. Indeed, it is possible that the results of these tests will be so negative that the whole proposal is discredited. But jobs will continue to vanish, and the political risk involved in creating a huge and resentful underclass of the unemployed is so great that something will have to be done about it. If it isn't UBI, it will have to be some other solution that maintains the incomes of the jobless at a level that allows them to lead a reasonably comfortable life without a job, and in a way that does not humiliate them.

> Hegel remarks somewhere that all facts and personages of great importance in world history occur, as it were, twice. He forgot to add: the first time as tragedy, the second as farce.
>
> Karl Marx, *The Eighteenth Brumaire of Louis Napoleon* (1852).

It's not always farce the second time. Sometimes it's horror. The nineteenth-century pogroms in Eastern

Europe were bad; the twentieth-century Holocaust was far worse. But while historical patterns do persist and repeat, for better or for worse, we are not trapped in an endlessly repeating cycle. Hegel did not really believe that; the mature Marx certainly didn't either (he was only thirty-four in 1852) — and neither should we.

When you are addressing a very large and contentious subject such as the future of politics in democratic societies, it's important to make your historical assumptions clear. Mine are as follows. I believe that human history is best seen as an experiment to determine whether a species that evolved to live in quite small groups (almost always less than one hundred people) can successfully live in societies many millions strong. These enormous societies are the basis of our civilisation and the source of all our technological prowess, but they are certainly not 'natural', and the question of how to run them has always been problematic.

The first solution was god-kings, strict, steep hierarchies, and universal militarisation. It was all a very long way from the egalitarian values of the little hunter-gatherer groups we had lived in for thousands of generations, but we did have the hierarchical reflexes of our more distant primate ancestors to draw on, so we managed to make it work. We *had* to make it work, because these new mass civilisations needed to be controlled and directed, and in the absence of mass media there was no possibility of doing it by consensus. Orders had to be given and obeyed.

The price our ancestors paid for civilisation was ten thousand years of tyranny, oppression, and slavery —

but it is quite clear that these institutions were always at odds with core human values. Almost all rulers were constrained by law and custom. Even several thousand years ago, some small city-states were experimenting with democracy. And, most significantly, the new mass religions that swept the world in the 'axial age' all emphasised the equality of the believers, and indeed of all mankind. Egalitarianism was utterly absent in the world these people lived in, but it lived on in their dreams.

And then, about two hundred and fifty years ago, we got mass media. The printing press had already been around for three centuries, but it had to wait for mass literacy to catch up. When it finally did, it became possible for the first time for societies millions strong to be on the same page. Debates about goals and values involving many or most adult members of the society suddenly became possible, and it turned out that they wanted their old egalitarian values back. It is no coincidence at all that the first society of more than a million people ever to achieve 50 per cent adult literacy — the Thirteen Colonies that became the United States — was also the first to have a successful democratic revolution and to design a political system based on equal rights for all its citizens. Well, all its white adult male citizens, anyway, but once the principle of equality has been accepted, the practice will generally follow eventually.

Many forms of Government have been tried, and will be tried in this world of sin and woe. No one pretends that democracy is perfect or all-wise. Indeed it has been said that democracy is the worst form of Government except for all those other forms that have been tried from time to time ...

Winston Churchill, House of Commons, 11 November 1947

Only a decade after the American Revolution came the far more radical French Revolution. (Literacy was above 70 per cent in Paris, although far lower in the rest of the country.) That revolution was then hijacked by a series of tyrants, of course, and the same has happened to some others since, but the principle of equality and the democratic system, however much abused in practice, are now the default political mode all over the world. History is *not* cyclical. There *is* such a thing as progress.

The extraordinary success of democracy owes nothing to the specific historical origins of these ideas in the European Enlightenment, nor should we accept the notion that the West got there first because it had ancient Greeks up its collective family tree. The West got there first because it was the first part of the world to achieve mass literacy, and the ideas spread to every corner of the world because they correspond to basic human values. And by a happy coincidence (or maybe it's more than that), democracy is the best political system for an era when mass societies must contend with enormous economic, technological, social, and environmental changes that are largely of their own making.

These changes, from climate change to artificial intelligence, are the unforeseen and usually unintended consequences of the industrial and scientific revolutions, but with hindsight you can see that they were also inevitable. The rise of democracy in this era was also inevitable, and it will be indispensable in coping with the changes, but its success is by no means guaranteed. It is easily subverted by old-fashioned populism, especially when that is supercharged by social media; and if we revert to the authoritarian nationalism that did such huge damage in the twentieth century, we will wreck the twenty-first as well. We may also lose the great gamble we unwittingly accepted when we began to develop a technological civilisation at the start of the industrial revolution two hundred and fifty years ago.

2

Don't touch that button!

If they do not now accept our terms they may expect a rain of ruin from the air, the like of which has never been seen on this earth.

> US President Harry S. Truman, 6 August 1945 (16 hours after the atomic bombing of Hiroshima)

North Korea best not make any more threats to the United States. They will be met with fire and fury like the world has never seen.

> US President Donald Trump, 9 August 2017, speaking to reporters at his golf club in Bedminster, New Jersey.

Truman's measured warning to Japan (followed three days later by a second atomic bomb on Nagasaki when Japan's military rulers refused to surrender), and Trump's off-the-cuff threats to North Korea seventy-two years later, are eerily similar in form, but they are very different in context. Truman was speaking at the culmination of the greatest war in history, with more than 40 million people already dead. Trump was making nuclear threats in a confrontation where nobody's been killed yet (though millions might be, almost all of them non-American) — and if you look at the video, he was clearly enjoying the moment.

The chaos of Donald Trump's White House, his visible contempt for the Republican leadership in Congress, and his famously short attention span all suggest that he will have only a limited impact on domestic affairs in the United States, but in foreign policy American presidents have virtually free rein. As a candidate he was isolationist, promising to cut back sharply on America's overseas commitments, and to a certain extent he has delivered on those promises as president. He has withdrawn from the Trans-Pacific Partnership trade agreement (TPP), probably killing it in the process (although Japan is trying hard to revive it in a shrunken form), and he has put its European equivalent, the Trans-Atlantic Trade and Investment Partnership (TTIP), on indefinite hold. He has pulled out of the Paris climate accord, and he threatens to end the North American Free Trade Agreement (NAFTA) if it is not rewritten to his liking. His attitude to America's most important alliance, the North Atlantic Treaty Organization (NATO), is ambivalent at best. But he has doubled down on America's overseas military commitments.

The [Iraq] war's a total disaster. It's a catastrophe …
How do they get out? They get out, that's how they get
out. Declare a victory and leave.

> Donald Trump with Wolf Blitzer, CNN Live, 16 March
> 2007

I will never send our finest into battle unless necessary,
and I mean absolutely necessary, and will only do so if
we have a plan for victory with a capital V. The world
must know that we do not go abroad in search of
enemies.

> Donald Trump, 27 April 2016[1]

Trump was quite right to condemn the foolish
and unnecessary wars launched by his Republican
predecessor, George W. Bush, but it took just a few
whiffs of the intoxicating air in the Oval Room for him
to be seduced into reinforcing those failures himself:
more troops for Afghanistan, more troops in Iraq, more
troops and a pointless cruise missile strike against Syria.
As he has said himself, 'I am the greatest hawk who
ever lived, a far greater hawk even than Bush. I am the
most militant military human being who ever lived.'[2]
His pugnacious character and the endless opportunities
to grandstand have also drawn him into a major and
potentially nuclear confrontation with North Korea, and
a close alliance with Saudi Arabia that could involve the
United States in a war with Iran. He has served a useful
purpose in alerting us to the anger of the 'left-behinds',
but he could also be the first man to start a nuclear war.

The Korean peninsula is the only part of the world where you can currently write a plausible scenario for the outbreak of a nuclear war, and it certainly wouldn't be North Korea that starts it. The North Korean regime is absolutely determined to have both nuclear weapons and the ability to deliver at least a few of them on the United States, but that is not because Kim Jong-un wants to attack the US. It is because he and his colleagues, like his father and his grandfather before them, want to deter the US from using nuclear weapons on North Korea. There has never been the slightest sign that Trump understands this basic fact.

As Russia's president, Vladimir Putin, said of the North Korean leaders in September 2017, 'They would rather eat grass than give up their nuclear programme.' Putin was consciously borrowing the phrase 'eat grass' from Pakistan's former prime minister Zulfikar Ali Bhutto, who said, 'We will eat grass, even go hungry, but we will get one of our own' after India exploded its first 'peaceful nuclear device' (that is, an atomic bomb) in 1974. If your adversary has nuclear weapons, you cannot afford not to have them — and the United States, not South Korea, is North Korea's main adversary in the Korean peninsula.

The United States has had nuclear weapons since before the 'Democratic People's Republic of Korea' (North Korea) even came into existence, and for all but the past dozen years of that time North Korea had none. There was no peace treaty at the end of the Korean War (1950–53), only an armistice, so the two Koreas are still technically at war — and the United States has never promised not to use nuclear weapons on North Korea if major fighting breaks out again in the Korean peninsula. Indeed, it has come close to using them there in the past.

During the Korean War (1950–53), General Douglas MacArthur, the American commander in the Far East, considered going nuclear on several occasions. In October 1950, after his forces had recovered from an initial defeat, overrun most of North Korea, and advanced almost all the way to the Chinese border, MacArthur was surprised (though he shouldn't have been) by a large Chinese force that counter-attacked from across the border. As American troops fled south in the 'Big Bug-Out', he came up with a cunning plan to stop the Chinese: 'It was my plan as our [troops retreated] to spread behind us — from the Sea of Japan to the Yellow Sea — a belt of radioactive cobalt. It could have been spread from wagons, carts, trucks, and planes … For at least 60 years there could have been no land invasion of Korea from the north. The enemy could not have marched across that radiated belt.'[3]

Like most American soldiers of his generation (he fought on the Western Front in the First World War), General MacArthur was simultaneously in awe of nuclear weapons and quite ignorant about the niggling details — such as the fact that there was not enough refined cobalt-60 in the world to carry out even one-hundredth of his plan. Later in the war, he at least contemplated the use of nuclear weapons on China, although there is no evidence that he ever recommended it to President Truman. The president ultimately dismissed him for insubordination, and it all happened a long time ago — but there can be no doubt that every generation of North Korean leaders and soldiers since then has been taught about MacArthur's plan. (The same goes for the Chinese.) Like the Pakistanis after India's first nuclear test, the North Koreans felt naked and utterly vulnerable until they got nukes of their own. It just took the North Koreans a lot longer to get there.

> The writer ... is not for the moment concerned about who will win the next war in which atomic bombs are used. Thus far the chief purpose of our military establishment has been to win wars. From now on its chief purpose must be to avert them. It can have almost no other useful purpose.
>
> Bernard Brodie, 1946[4]

I interviewed Bernard Brodie in the last year of his life, and he was filled with remorse for the many years he had spent playing with concepts of 'limited' nuclear war in the 1950s and 1960s, but he was right at the first and he was right again by the end. In the winter of 1945–46, only months after the atomic bombs on Hiroshima and Nagasaki, Brodie led a group of young American academics in a study of what would be the appropriate strategy for a world of nuclear-armed great powers, and they concluded that the only useful role for nuclear weapons was deterrence. Fighting a nuclear war would cause death and damage on an unthinkable scale, far exceeding the importance of whatever issues were at stake, and so American nuclear weapons had to remain unused — but they had to remain in existence, protected from a surprise attack, to deter other similarly armed countries from launching a nuclear 'first strike' against the United States. Brodie was the father of the deterrence theory that now rules strategic thinking in all the nuclear-weapons powers — but it was at least fifteen years before his own country adopted his ideas.

This was only to be expected, because until the first Soviet nuclear test in 1949 the United States was the only nuclear-weapons power in a world of conventional weapons, and even down to the end of the 1950s America's nuclear weapons were so numerous and its delivery systems so superior that it could effectively 'win' a nuclear war against the Soviet Union. This was what seduced Brodie in mid-career into exploring theories of 'limited' nuclear war that would exploit this transitory American dominance in these weapons, to his later regret. By the mid-1960s, however, both the United States and the Soviet Union had large numbers of unstoppable ballistic missiles, and the doctrine of mutual deterrence had been accepted by pretty much the entire American strategic community.

The strategic relationship between the United States and North Korea as regards nuclear weapons has not yet reached this relatively stable end-point. North Korea's nuclear weapons are new, and perhaps not very reliable. They are certainly few in number. The same applies to North Korean intercontinental ballistic missiles (ICBMs), which are in their initial flight-test phase and have only recently achieved the range needed to reach all parts of the United States. So there is not yet full mutual deterrence between the two countries, and the United States, as in the early days of the Cold War vis-a-vis its Soviet opponent, does have the option of launching a massive nuclear first strike against North Korea that might destroy all its nuclear weapons and missiles, and decapitate its leadership. Or it might fail to achieve these objectives — the outcome is inherently unpredictable — and one or several North Korean nuclear weapons might survive and explode on American soil. A similar level of uncertainty was enough to prevent the United States from seriously considering a nuclear first strike against the Soviet Union even in the 1950s, and it should have the same effect today. It would take a very rash or ignorant leader to take such a gamble — but such leaders do exist. Some of them sound like angry children in the playground.

> The United States has great strength and patience, but if it is forced to defend itself or its allies, we will have no choice but to totally destroy North Korea. Rocket Man is on a suicide mission for himself and for his regime.
>
> Donald Trump speaking at the UN General Assembly, 19 September 2017

> [Trump] is surely a rogue and a gangster fond of playing with fire, rather than a politician … I will surely and definitely tame the mentally deranged US dotard with fire.
>
> Kim Jong-un's personal response, 21 September 2017[5]

Kim Jong-un of North Korea, who is obviously a
madman who doesn't mind starving or killing his
people, will be tested like never before!
     Trump tweet, 3.28 am, 22 September 2017

The vast majority of Americans are blissfully unaware
that there is any hypocrisy involved in demanding that
North Korea refrain from getting what the United States
has had for the past seventy-three years, and the US
government is equally oblivious to the double standards
on display. US Secretary of State Rex Tillerson was
being entirely sincere when he said that North Korea's
ICBM test 'represents a new escalation of the threat to
the United States, our allies and partners, the region,
and the world'. Wrong, but entirely sincere.

The United States has at least a hundred times as
many nuclear weapons as North Korea, and delivery
vehicles that are at least two technological generations
further down the road. It also has a clearly stated policy
that it might use nuclear weapons first in a conflict. In
practice, it would only ever exercise this option against
relatively small and weak countries; it would never launch
a first strike against a fully fledged nuclear-weapons
power such as Russia or China, because the retaliation
would cause massive devastation in the United States.
Unfortunately for North Korea, it is a relatively small
and weak country. Pyongyang is obviously well aware of
this, and quite frightened by it. It blusters and lies a lot,
partly because it is so frightened and partly because that
is the house style anyway, but it would never launch a
nuclear first strike against the United States or its allies.

That really would be a suicide mission.

North Korea will probably have ICBMs that can reach big American cities with a fair degree of accuracy in a year or two if it keeps up its current pace of development and testing. That would buy it a limited degree of safety from an American nuclear attack, because one or more of its missiles might survive a US first strike and be able to carry out a 'revenge from the grave'. But even full-range nuclear-tipped ICBMs would still not allow North Korea to launch a nuclear attack on America (or on South Korea, which has an American nuclear guarantee) without being exterminated in an immediate, massive nuclear counter-strike. So you can probably trust the North Korean regime not to do anything so terminally stupid — unless people like Kim Jong-un are literally crazy.

That's why American diplomats work so hard to convince everybody else that the North Korean regime really is frothing mad, impervious to logic, a threat to the whole world, and not even interested in self-preservation. Only then can they argue that the North Koreans should be denied nuclear weapons, although Americans, Russians, Chinese, British, French, Israelis, Indians, and Pakistanis can be trusted with them. There is no evidence that the North Koreans really are crazy. In the sixty-five years since the end of the Korean War, they have never risked a war, and they are extremely unlikely to do so now. And while there is a leader in Washington at the moment whose taste in personal abuse rivals that of the North Korean leader, people want to believe that there is enough adult supervision in the White House to avoid any fatal mistakes on the American side either.

Washington gossip is often just wishful thinking, but reports began surfacing in late 2017 that the US Secretary of Defense, General James Mattis, the National Security Advisor, General H.R McMaster, and Trump's Chief of Staff, General John Kelly, have made a secret pact that they would never be abroad at the same time. That would be comforting if it were true, because it would mean that at least one very senior military officer would always be in the country to monitor orders coming from the White House, and countermand them if necessary. Unfortunately, there are two reasons to doubt this. First, it's only a rumour. Second, only Mattis is in the chain of command, and any countermanding orders he might issue would probably arrive too late.

'The president has absolute authority, unilateral power, to order the use of nuclear weapons,' says Bruce Blair, who was once a launch-control officer for Minuteman ICBMs, and later founded Global Zero, a group that advocates eliminating nuclear weapons entirely. The nuclear codes that the president would punch into the 'football' (the device controlling nuclear-weapons launches that an aide always carries around close to the president) are 'the length of a tweet. It would take them one or two minutes to format and transmit that directly down the chain of command to the executing commanders of the underground launch centers, the submarines, and the bombers.' Mattis and various other generals would get the order, too, of course — but, as Blair says, 'If they felt that it was a really bad call or illegal, and they wanted to try to override it, they could try to transmit a termination order, but it would be too late.'[6]

This bizarre situation dates back to the early days of the Cold War, when both the United States and the Soviet Union had 'launch-on-warning' policies because they feared that an enemy first strike could destroy all of their own nuclear weapons and leave them helpless. 'Use 'em or lose 'em' was the mantra, so the US and Soviet leaders had the authority to launch their missiles in minutes. Later on, both countries buried their ballistic missiles in underground silos or hid them in submerged submarines so they could not lose them in a surprise attack. They no longer had to launch on a warning that might be false: if there really was an attack, they could ride it out and retaliate afterwards. But the US never bothered to take back the president's 'instant launch' authority. Donald Trump really could make a nuclear first strike on North Korea all on his own — and Kim Jong-un could presumably do the same thing in the other direction. On this vital issue, there is no 'adult supervision'.

We can't blame Trump for being president when the North Korean nuclear and missile programmes finally came to fruition. We can regret that it was Trump, because his predecessors, both Republican and Democratic, understood that if sanctions didn't succeed in stopping North Korea, there was nothing further to be done unless they were willing to attack North Korea with nuclear weapons themselves. Trump sometimes seems not to understand that this is a dreadful option, as he has been quoted on a number of occasions asking his advisers why the United States doesn't use them, but it makes no sense to fight a real nuclear war now in order to prevent an imaginable but highly unlikely nuclear war sometime in the future.

We live in dangerous times, but there is probably not going to be a Second Korean War. North Korea will probably get an effective nuclear deterrent force in the end, and we will all probably learn to live with it — just as we learned to live with mutual US–Russian nuclear deterrence, mutual US–Chinese nuclear deterrence, and mutual Indian–Pakistani nuclear deterrence. And if, by great misfortune, there should be renewed war in the Korean peninsula and nuclear weapons are used, it would not be the continent-killing disaster that loomed over everybody in the decades of the Cold War. It would, however, be an unlimited calamity for Koreans, both North and South, of whom millions might die, and a very frightening time for everybody else.

> The United States and the United Nations Security Council sought, over many years, to stop Iran's pursuit of nuclear weapons with a wide array of strong economic sanctions. But the previous administration lifted these sanctions, just before what would have been the total collapse of the Iranian regime, through the deeply controversial 2015 nuclear deal with Iran. This deal is known as the Joint Comprehensive Plan of Action, or JCPOA. As I have said many times, the Iran deal was one of the worst and most one-sided transactions the United States has ever entered into.
>
> Donald Trump speech, 13 October 2017

Trump's response to North Korea's nuclear and ballistic missile tests may be reckless and bellicose, but he is at least responding to a real problem. In trying to destroy the JCPOA, signed by all the world's nuclear-armed great powers plus Germany in 2015, he is creating a problem where none existed before. (And no, the Iranian regime was not on the brink of collapse when the deal was signed.)

The escalating economic sanctions that the UN Security Council imposed on Iran after it refused to suspend its uranium-enrichment activities in 1996 culminated successfully in Iran's signature of the JCPOA treaty in 2015, but what that deal stopped was not Iran's pursuit of actual nuclear weapons. That had already ceased in 2003. Instead it obliged Iran to abandon, at least for ten years, its attempts to achieve what is known as 'threshold' status: the technical ability to break out of the Nuclear Non-Proliferation Treaty's constraints and develop a nuclear-weapons capability quickly — within one or two years — were one of the country's nuclear-armed near neighbours to suddenly turn hostile. Those neighbours include Pakistan (which shares a common border with Iran), Israel, Russia, and the United States' Fifth Fleet (based in Bahrain).

In most parts of the world, threshold status is not a big deal. Germany, Japan, Argentina, Brazil, and the Netherlands are all threshold nuclear-weapons powers: they could produce enough enriched uranium for a bomb in a year, although it would take them several years to produce an actual weapon. Canada, Belgium, Italy, Spain, and Australia are in the same category, though it would take a little longer, and South Africa presumably retains a threshold capability, although it has dismantled the nuclear weapons it built in the late apartheid years. So why hasn't the UN Security Council brought sanctions against them, too? Because their enrichment facilities are perfectly legal under the Nuclear Non-Proliferation Treaty, which they have all signed. Iran's enrichment facilities are equally legal, and it has also signed the NPT. Countries that exercise their right to enrich uranium have to allow inspections by the International Atomic Energy Agency (IAEA) to ensure that they are not enriching it to weapons grade, and for the past decade and a half, Iran has abided by the letter of those rules.

However, the United States government does not trust the Iranians. Even more to the point, Israel does not trust them, and Israel has great, perhaps decisive, influence in Washington on this question. So the United States demanded that Iran stop enriching uranium even to the level (2.5 per cent pure) that is needed for nuclear-power reactors. If Iran could do even a little bit of enrichment, Washington argued, that would give it the ability to enrich uranium all the way up to weapons grade (90 per cent pure), and to make nuclear weapons sometime in the future. In other words, Iran would have to accept special constraints, well beyond the NPT rules, because it was untrustworthy. The Iranians were understandably outraged by this, but there is a good deal of history here: Iran *has* sought nuclear weapons in the past.

Shortly after the Islamic Revolution of 1978–79

brought Ayatollah Khomeini to power in Tehran, Saddam Hussein's Iraq invaded Iran in 1980 with tacit encouragement from the United States. Both countries assumed that Iran's shaky new revolutionary regime would crack quickly, but the war turned into an eight-year battle of attrition in which more than a million soldiers died in the trenches. Poison gas was used extensively by the Iraqi side, and by the end, in 1988, the US Defense Intelligence Agency was giving the Iraqi intelligence services detailed information, including satellite imagery, on the deployments and movements of all Iranian combat units. This gave the Iraqi air force 'targeting packages', in the words of retired US Air Force Col. Rick Francona, who was a military attaché in Baghdad during the 1988 strikes, that included sarin (nerve gas). 'The Iraqis never told us that they intended to use nerve gas,' said Francona. 'They didn't have to. We already knew.'[7]

The Iranians knew that Iraq was also working on nuclear weapons, and had no doubt that it would use them as soon as it got them. By 1984, Iranian leaders were so concerned about an Iraqi nuclear bomb that they authorised a comparable Iranian nuclear-weapons programme, but that lost speed and may even been shut down entirely for a time after the end of the war in 1988, or at the latest when the Iraqi programme was dismantled by UN inspectors after the Gulf War of 1990–91. However, Iran resumed development work on nuclear weapons in 1998, after Pakistan tested six nuclear bombs in three days.

Pakistani regimes, whether civilian or military, are

DON'T TOUCH THAT BUTTON! 47

not particularly hostile to Iran as a rule, but the Pakistani military, almost uniquely among the armed forces of Muslim-majority countries, allows Islamists to rise to high rank. The possibility that extreme Islamist officers might someday seize power in Islamabad is therefore never absent from Iranian calculations. As fanatical Sunnis, those officers would be deeply hostile to Shia Iran, and now they would have nuclear weapons as well. Iran might need a nuclear deterrent against Pakistan at some future time, the thinking went, so it should at least have a threshold nuclear capability, even though it did not need the actual weapons immediately.

That drive for a threshold capability lasted until 2002, when The National Council of Resistance in Iran, the political wing of the terrorist organisation Mujahideen-e Khalq (MeK), revealed that Iran was building secret nuclear facilities near Natanz and Arak. (The information may have been leaked to them by US intelligence.) The International Atomic Energy Agency (IAEA) investigated, and in mid-2003 Tehran agreed to suspend its uranium enrichment activities and ratify an additional protocol requiring Iran to provide an expanded declaration of its nuclear activities and granting the IAEA broader rights of access to sites in the country. That was the end of the 'threshold' programme, and in November 2007 all sixteen US intelligence agencies contributed to a National Intelligence Estimate saying that Iran had stopped work on nuclear weapons in 2003. Everybody except Israeli Prime Minister Binyamin Netanyahu agrees that it has not resumed work since.

At no time have Iran's nuclear-weapons ambitions had anything to do with Israel. The Islamic Republic of Iran strongly disapproves of Israel's actions, of course. In 2005, one president, the obnoxious and bombastic Mahmoud Ahmadinejad, even quoted the late Ayatollah Khomeini's religious judgement that 'this regime occupying Jerusalem must vanish from the page of time'. But contrary to persistent Israeli propaganda, Ahmadinejad never said that Israel should be wiped from the map, let alone that Iran could or should be the country that made it happen. In fact, most Iranians do not worry at all about Israel's hundreds of nuclear weapons and multiple means of delivery, against which Iran has no plausible defence. That reality has been a constant since all but the oldest Iranians were children, and the unspoken assumption is that the Israelis are a relatively predictable and unthreatening enemy. Or at least that was the case until Netanyahu started trying to persuade the United States to join Israel in a joint attack on all of Iran's nuclear facilities.

He got nowhere with president Barack Obama in that enterprise, and even Donald Trump does not say that Iran is now working on nuclear weapons. The conclusion of the JCPOA treaty in 2015 imposed severe restrictions for at least ten years on Iranian activities that might be related to nuclear weapons, and gave unprecedented access to IAEA inspectors to ensure that the Iranians are complying with them. In return, Iran has been released from all UN sanctions, presumably to the ultimate benefit of Iran's sagging economy.

Netanyahu continues to rail against the deal, but his

own soldiers and intelligence services disagree with him. General Gadi Eizenkot, the chief of the Israel General Staff, said in 2016 that, 'Without a doubt the nuclear deal between Iran and the West is a historic turning point. It is a big change in terms of the direction that Iran was headed, and in the way that we saw things.' Ephraim Halevy, the former chief of Israel's foreign intelligence agency, Mossad, issued a similar assessment: 'I believe this agreement closes the roads and blocks the road to Iranian nuclear military capabilities for at least a decade. And I believe that the arrangements that have been agreed between the parties are such that [they] give us a credible answer to the Iranian military threat, at least for a decade, if not longer.'[8] Yet Netanyahu still insists that it is a 'historic mistake', and demands that the deal be cancelled and the sanctions restored. It is hard to see how doing that would be beneficial for Israel, since it would free Iran to resume work on nuclear weapons at once if it was so inclined, but Netanyahu's motives may have more to do with Israel's domestic politics than with strategic considerations.

President Trump's decision to 'decertify' the JCPOA agreement, which he excoriates as the 'worst deal ever', is equally hard to explain. He refers vaguely to minor Iranian 'violations' of the deal, but the IAEA and all the other signatories maintain that Iran is in compliance with all the terms. He complains that Iran is breaking the 'spirit of the deal', citing its testing of long-range ballistic missiles and its continuing support for the Syrian regime, the Hezbollah party and militia in Lebanon, and Hamas in the Gaza Strip, but the JCPOA did not address those issues at all. As a man with much business experience, good and bad, Trump must know that if it isn't in the contract, it's not part of the deal. Even his own secretary of defense, former general Jim Mattis, has told Congress that the deal is in the national-security interest of the United States, and still Trump persists. Why? Perhaps he has been persuaded by Saudi Arabia to take Riyadh's side in its rivalry with Iran for the role of dominant regional power in the Middle East, but Trump was already promising to break the deal during the election campaign, long before he went to Riyadh. Absent any other plausible explanation, the suspicion must be that it is just part of his obsessive campaign to eradicate every trace of his predecessor's political legacy. The Iran deal was Barack Obama's greatest diplomatic accomplishment, so it must be destroyed.

It will not be easily destroyed. Britain, France, Germany, Russia, China, and the European Union have all said that Iran is observing the agreement in good faith, and that they will not revive sanctions against Iran even if the United States does. Iran has said that it will stick by the agreement so long as the other parties do, and indeed it would be foolish to do otherwise. The Europeans, however, might find it hard to stick by that decision in the long run, because any European companies trading with Iran might find themselves banned from trading with the United States, a far bigger market. Even then it would be in Iran's interest to stay with the deal, but at some point national pride might overcome self-interest.

I have got serious reservations about Donald Trump as President of the United States. The biggest threat the world faces is how we all adjust to the progressive withdrawal of responsible American leadership and the network of alliances that America maintained with Europe, with Asian countries and the partnerships they had across the region.

Sir John Sawyers, former head of the British intelligence agency MI6[9]

A Second Korean War would be a calamity for the Koreans, millions of whom might be killed. If nuclear weapons were used (as they probably would be), it would make the rest of the world a more dangerous place, but it would not become a global catastrophe unless the Chinese were also drawn into the fighting. The odds on that are impossible to calculate, but it is unlikely.

Apart from Korea, the international damage that the Trump administration can do is fairly limited. American withdrawal from the JCPOA agreement would not necessarily lead to Iranian nuclear weapons, and Trump is the least likely American politician to get into a confrontation with Russia. (Indeed, his links with Russia may yet prove to be his downfall.) Even in Syria, where the US army and air force are operating in the same battle space as the Russian air force and Iranian militias, much care is being taken on both sides to avoid misunderstandings and potential confrontations, and in any case the effective collapse of Islamic State means that the worst of the fighting is probably over.

It is unnerving to have an erratic narcissist like Donald Trump in such a powerful position, but most other major countries are still committed to the arrangements that have kept the peace between the great powers for so long. No guarantees, of course, but Trump's time in office could pass without doing any irreversible damage to the current international system.

The greater concern is the fact, or at least the perception, that the world is drifting back into the ultra-nationalist, authoritarian political style — 'populism', in a word — that we last saw in the 1930s. There is much more to be said about this, and in particular about the viability of democracy, but first we should look at the practical impact of populism on the politics of one of the oldest democracies: the United Kingdom.

3

The EU and Brexit: immigrants or jobs?

> If there had been no EU to join, eastern Europe would
> be a string of pre-2014 Ukraines.
>> John Lichfield, *The Independent*, 23 March 2014

It is perfectly possible to claim, as various Brexiteers have done in the United Kingdom, that the European Union is far more ambitious and intrusive than the organisation that would be required just to administer a Europe-wide free-trade area, but it was never intended to be merely a trading bloc. Its founders saw it as a vital bulwark against a return of the dictatorships, and even more importantly against a resurgence of the rivalries between the European great powers that had fuelled most of the big wars of the previous four hundred years. Get them all in the same club, and maybe they won't want to fight any more.

This is not the only reason that no great power has

directly fought any other great power for seventy-three years now: some of the credit must go to the fear of nuclear weapons, and some more to the new international rules embodied in the United Nations. But it certainly helped, and it's hard to deny that the EU was indispensable in offering a safe haven to all the would-be democracies of post-communist eastern Europe after 1989. Membership not only involved the promise of prosperity, but an obligation to uphold democratic principles and the rule of law. A mere free-trade area would not have done that, and Europe (and maybe the world) would be a much uglier place if the EU did not exist.

> The people have spoken. I think the EU is going to break up.
>
> Donald Trump, interview in *The Times* about the UK referendum, 25 June 2016

> You look at the European Union and it's Germany. Basically a vehicle for Germany. That's why I thought the UK was so smart in getting out.
>
> Donald Trump, interview in *The Times*, 16 January 2017

> The EU, I'm totally in favour of it. I think it's wonderful, if they're happy. If they're happy — I'm in favour of it.
>
> Donald Trump, *The Independent*, 23 February 2017

There's no point in trying to make sense of it all. He changes with the weather. But the perception in the

EU is that Trump is hostile to the organisation's very existence, and it had enough troubles already. One-third of French voters supported the anti-EU National Front in the presidential run-off election of May 2017, and Germany's strongly pro-EU chancellor, Angela Merkel, saw her party's vote drop by 8 per cent to less than a third of the total in an September 2017 election that also saw the Eurosceptic, anti-immigrant Alternative for Germany Party (AfD) win one-eighth of the votes and gain seats in parliament for the first time. In Italy, the Five-Star Movement, also sceptical about the EU, is running neck-and-neck with the Democratic Party in the opinion polls, with an election imminent. The Spanish government is distracted by the attempted secession of Catalonia. Poland and Hungary are both governed by nationalist parties whose authoritarian style and strongly anti-immigrant and anti-Muslim bias put them at odds with the EU more often than not. And, of course, the United Kingdom is flouncing out of the EU, impelled by a wave of 'Little Englander' nationalism.

The twenty-eight-country union has clearly seen better times, and its ambitions for an 'ever-closer union' are on hold for the moment, if not forever, but most of its troubles do not derive from the same sources as those that put Donald Trump in the presidency in the United States. Apart from Britain, and to a lesser extent France, there is little evidence that working-class voters in deprived post-industrial areas in Europe voted differently than they had in previous elections. Immigration as a hot-button topic was more prominent everywhere than it was in the US election because of the big surge in Syrian and other mostly Muslim refugees (1.3 million) who arrived in European countries in 2015. The fact that the EU asked its eastern European members to take some of the refugees caused particularly strong resentment there, mainly because these countries had almost no previous experience of immigration, and local nationalist politicians ruthlessly exploited the issue. The spectacular rise in Germany of the AfD (which has some neo-Nazi links) was largely due to its strong showing in former East Germany, where employment and wages remain sharply lower than in the rest of the country, even a quarter-century after reunification. If there was an overall 'Trump effect' underlying all this, it was remarkably well hidden.

We must build a kind of United States of Europe ... (and) we must begin now. In these present days we dwell strangely and precariously under the shield and protection of the atomic bomb. The atomic bomb is still only in the hands of a State and nation which we know will never use it except in the cause of right and freedom. But it may well be that in a few years this awful agency of destruction will be widespread and the catastrophe following from its use by several warring nations will not only bring to an end all that we call civilisation, but may possibly disintegrate the globe itself ... Our constant aim must be to build and fortify the strength of the United Nations Organisation. Under and within that world concept, we must re-create the European family in a regional structure called, it may be, the United States of Europe. The first step is to form a Council of Europe. If at first all the States of Europe are not willing or able to join the Union, we must nevertheless proceed to assemble and combine those who will and those who can.

Winston Churchill, University of Zurich, 19 September 1946

It took a while, although the logic of a united Europe was compelling. If you don't want a Third World War fought with nuclear weapons, you have to deal with the structures that produced the first two, and the proximate cause of both of them was the ambitions and fears of the rival European great powers. But the United Kingdom, although it had been one of those warring great powers for 400 years, saw itself as something apart: Churchill wasn't planning for Britain to join this new organisation he was advocating.

That attitude persisted in the United Kingdom for a long time. Although Britain's century as the world's greatest power had expired long before, it still had its empire (or most of it), and it had a 'special relationship' with the United States, the other great English-speaking country, that it valued more highly than its European ties. The Council of Europe was created in 1949, and its first venture into the real world of economic integration was the foundation of the European Coal and Steel Community in 1951. That expanded into the much more comprehensive European Economic Community (popularly known as the Common Market) in 1957, but the United Kingdom still did not consider joining.

By 1961 the EEC was growing a lot faster economically than the UK, and the economic argument succeeded where the geopolitical argument for joining had failed. London finally realised that its interest was best served by being part of this new trading bloc, and applied for membership — which was vetoed by French president Charles de Gaulle in 1963 on the grounds that Britain did not have 'a European vocation'. De Gaulle vetoed a second British attempt to join in 1967, and it was only finally allowed to join years after he had resigned. But he was right about the British attitude: it was love-hate from the start.

Having finally joined the EEC under Conservative prime minister Edward Heath in 1973, the United Kingdom demanded a renegotiation of its terms of membership and held an in/out referendum on EEC membership under a Labour government two years later. It demanded another renegotiation of its membership terms under Conservative prime minister Margaret Thatcher in 1984. It insisted on opting out of the planned single currency when the countries of the European Union (as it now styled itself) signed the Treaty of Maastricht in 1993. And another Conservative prime minister, David Cameron, demanded *another* renegotiation of the terms of membership, in what is now called the European Union in 2013, and promised *yet another* referendum once the results were known.

If you were looking for a single word to describe this behaviour, 'ambivalent' would certainly spring to mind. 'Petulant' also has a strong claim. But why, out of the European Union's now twenty-eight countries, has

Britain always been the most disaffected one?

All the countries on the west coast of Europe lost their overseas empires in the decades after the Second World War, and Britain is not the only one to cling to delusions of grandeur in the aftermath. France, too, has a highly inflated view of its own importance. But the French understand the cost of European disunity much better than the British, because they have paid a higher price for it.

It has to do with the fact that Britain is an island. Almost every other European country except Switzerland and Sweden has seen serious fighting on its own soil in the past hundred years. Many of them have seen it several times, and about half of them have been partly or wholly occupied by foreign troops for long periods. By contrast, Britain has not been successfully invaded for almost a thousand years.

Britain is not alone in seeing the follies of the EU bureaucracy and resenting the cost of the compromises that have to be made to keep the enterprise alive. It *is* alone, or almost alone, in seeing European unity purely as an optional project, to be reassessed from time to time by calculating its economic benefits and weighing them against its political and emotional costs for Britain.

Emotional costs? Yes, and this is where the petulance comes from. There is a fantasy, still quite prevalent in England, that the country could have a much more satisfying future as a fully independent player unshackled from the dull and stodgy European Union, living by its wits as a swashbuckling global trader. To which one can only say: *Good luck with that*.

If this were all that is going on, other people in other countries would not be paying the Brexit phenomenon much attention. 'Middle-Sized Country Makes Large Mistake: not many hurt elsewhere' is not a very exciting headline. The interest lies in the possibility (or rather the fear) that the outburst of populist anger that led to the Brexit phenomenon will not be confined to Britain — and indeed we already have Donald Trump's astonishing rise to power in the United States to underline that fear. So it's worth spending some time on what actually happened in the United Kingdom, bearing always in mind that it could just be a local aberration.

> There's no such thing as society. There are individual men and women and there are families … It is our duty to look after ourselves (first) and then, also, to look after our neighbours.
> Prime Minister Margaret Thatcher, 1987

> If you believe you're a citizen of the world, you're a citizen of nowhere.
> Prime Minister Theresa May, 2017

Whoever Britain's third female prime minister should turn out to be, she's almost bound to be nicer than the first two. It would be hard to beat them on the negative-empathy front. But there is a significant distinction between these two women, Conservative prime ministers though they both were.

Margaret Thatcher was a disciple of Hayek and

the Chicago School, and her politics was the right-wing, 'small government' economic orthodoxy of the Anglosphere in the 1980s. She did not love the European Economic Community, but she recognised its importance as Britain's major trading partner. Indeed, she was the moving force behind the creation of the EU's 'single market', consolidated in 1993, that removed most of the non-tariff barriers to trade among EU members (at the cost of some extra 'red tape' to ensure that all EU members complied with the same quality and safety standards in their products).

Thirty years later, Theresa May is not greatly interested in that arcane old stuff about the economy. Her politics is nationalist, even tribal. Her priorities are preserving the English 'national identity' from erosion by too many immigrants, and recovering 'British sovereignty' (presuming that it has been lost) from Brussels and the European Court of Justice. Or at least those are the values she adopted in order to become prime minister in the aftermath of the 'Leave' victory in the Brexit referendum of June 2016, and she has ruthlessly subordinated the United Kingdom's economic interests to those higher goals. She is definitely the right prime minister for Brexit, if you like that sort of thing.

Yet it is typical of the haphazard, almost accidental, nature of the 2016 vote to leave the EU that Theresa May did not campaign for Brexit in the referendum. She kept a very low profile during the campaign, hoping to keep her position as home secretary in prime minister David Cameron's government if Brexit lost, but positioning herself to switch sides and emerge as a leading candidate for the prime ministership if Brexit won and Cameron was forced to resign. When she did speak (in private), she warned against the dangers of leaving the EU. Speaking to the staff of the Goldman Sachs investment bank in London at a closed meeting on 26 May 2016, one month before the referendum, she said:

> I think the economic arguments are clear. I think being part of a 500-million[-person] trading bloc is significant for us. I think … that one of the issues is that a lot of people will invest here in the UK because it is *the UK in Europe* [my italics]. If we were not in Europe, I think there would be firms and companies who would be looking to say, do they need to develop a mainland European presence rather than a UK presence? So I think there are definite benefits for us in economic terms.[1]

But Brexit won, and Theresa May trimmed her sails to catch the new wind. Cameron had given his cabinet ministers permission to campaign for either side, but he led the Remain campaign himself, and quit immediately as soon as the Leavers won. Despite the allegedly consultative nature of the referendum and the narrowness of the Brexit victory — 51.9 per cent Leave, 48.1 per cent Remain — the result was interpreted by the Conservative Party as an irrevocable decision that required a new prime minister and cabinet dedicated to carrying out the 'national will'.

The Conservative members of parliament who

had led the Brexit campaign, Boris Johnson and Michael Gove, were so astonished by their success (and in Johnson's case at least, so terrified by it), that they had not prepared any follow-on campaign for the party leadership in the unlikely event of a victory, and in less than three weeks May had snatched the prime ministership against feeble opposition. To do so, however, she had to become the hardest-line Brexiteer of them all — which also means a hard-line English nationalist.

English nationalism is a strange, awkward beast that has only recently emerged from its long submersion in the broader context of a British national identity: it's only in the past two decades that the English flag, the cross of St. George, has been on display even at football matches. The other three nations of the United Kingdom — Wales, Scotland, and Northern Ireland — have always had their own identities, and latterly, in Scotland's case, even an active separatist movement seeking Scottish independence. For most English people, however, 'English' and 'British' were virtually synonyms. They were, after all, 90 per cent of the British population.

The end of the British Empire was probably bound to be accompanied by the gradual re-emergence of an explicitly English identity. It took two or three decades, but it's been back since the 1990s — and whereas the other British nationalisms mostly define themselves against the English (Northern Ireland is a more complex case), English nationalism naturally defined itself against the larger 'European' identity that the country had also taken on when it joined the EU in 1973. English nationalists who really put their hearts into it (most people didn't) became Europhobes who saw the EU as a monolithic threat to their own identity and traditions, even though it actually accommodates several dozen other national identities and traditions with a fair degree of success. And the Europhobes, as conservatives and traditionalists, found a natural home in the right wing of the Conservative Party (still familiarly known by its 17th-century name, the Tories).

That is not to say that the Conservative Party as a whole was Europhobic. On the contrary, it was the Tories under Edward Heath who led the United Kingdom into the Common Market in 1973, and every subsequent Tory prime minister, down to and including David Cameron in 2010–16, defended British membership of the organisation. Nor was Labour, the other major party, always pro-EU: until the mid-1990s, the Labour Party's left wing always included a strong anti-EU faction, although their motivation was less English nationalism than hostility to all 'capitalist' institutions and a preference for building 'socialism in one country'. But by the 21st century both major British parties were generally in favour of British membership of the EU.

There continued to be a significant faction of Europhobe fanatics on the right wing of the Conservative Party, however, and from time to time these 'head-bangers' (as they were known to their fellow Tories of more moderate views) would launch failed rebellions against the Conservative Party leadership. This was more a nuisance than a genuine threat, but the first prime ministership of David Cameron in 2010–15 also saw the rise of a single-issue nationalist party, the United Kingdom Independence Party (UKIP), that was taking many more votes from the Conservatives than from Labour. The Conservatives were already in a coalition with the smaller Liberal Democratic Party, as they had not managed to win a parliamentary majority by themselves in the 2010 election. With the continuing rise of UKIP, they faced the threat of not being the largest single party either after the 2015 election. So David Cameron, though personally a strong supporter of British membership in the EU, had a bright idea.

In January 2013, Cameron announced that he would hold an in/out referendum on British membership of the EU *after* the 2015 election. That would shut up his own head-bangers in parliament and stop them from defecting to UKIP. It would also steal UKIP's thunder and stop anti-EU Conservative voters from defecting. Yet in all probability, he felt, he would never have to hold the referendum, because few people expected the Conservatives to win a majority in the 2015 election. The polls all suggested that Cameron would have to form another coalition with the Liberal Democrats after the election. The Lib Dems would then veto the referendum for him (sparing him the wrath of his own right wing), as they had never made any promises of their own about a referendum, and did not want one.

And if, somehow, despite all these calculations, Cameron did end up having to hold the referendum he had promised, it would still come out all right in the end, because the British people were not so stupid that more than half of them would vote to wreck their own economy. What could possibly go wrong?

> Perhaps it was always impossible to unite Great Britain with the continent. Naive to reconcile the legal system of Napoleon with the common law of the British Empire. Perhaps it was never meant to be.
>
> But our predecessors should never be blamed for having tried. Never. It's as important in politics as it is in life: to try new partnerships, new horizons, to reach out to each other, on the other side of the Channel.
>
> I am also sure that — one day or another — there will be a young man or woman who will try again, who will lead Britain into the European family once again. A young generation that will see Brexit for what it really is: a catfight in the Conservative party that got out of hand, a loss of time, a waste of energy, stupidity.
>
> Guy Verhofstadt, chief EU Brexit negotiator, speaking in the European Parliament, 5 April 2017

Verhofstadt's speech sounds like a valediction, which is a bit premature. It is not yet certain that the United Kingdom will crash out of the European Union in a 'hard Brexit' with no safety net, although that is what Prime Minister May was threatening when Verhofstadt spoke. It might end up being a 'soft Brexit' that leaves Britain in some sort of customs union with the EU, maybe even with some access to the 'single market', although that would require British concessions on topics such as the free movement of people that remain red lines for May at the time of writing. But leaving the EU is unquestionably an act of self-harm that will make the United Kingdom significantly poorer than if it stayed, and with no net gain in real freedom of action in the wider world as compensation for its losses. So why did slightly over half of the British voters who turned out in June 2016 choose to leave?

Not slightly over half of the entire adult population, of course — there were the usual no-shows on polling day, and the people who voted to 'Leave' were only 34.7 per cent of the eligible voters in the country. But there's no point in complaining about that: as the French say, 'The absent are always wrong.' No point, either, in complaining about the narrowness of the margin of victory for the 'Leave'. Cameron was so confident of winning that he didn't bother to impose any conditions of the sort that are often placed on referendums that might involve enormous changes and determine the fate of an entire country: minimum turn-out requirements, a 55 per cent or 60 per cent majority, etc. Brexit won, and that's that.

But the way the vote split demographically is very instructive. Almost two-thirds (64 per cent) of the voters over 65 years old supported the 'Leave' side; almost three-quarters (71 per cent) of the under-25s backed 'Remain'. In terms of social class, people in the highest categories (AB) voted two-to-one for Remain; people in the lowest categories (C2DE) voted two-to-one for Leave.

There was an even sharper distinction in education:

68 per cent of university graduates voted to Remain; 70 per cent of those with junior matriculation (GCSEs) or less voted to Leave. Households earning over £60,000 a year voted 65 per cent–35 per cent to Remain; households earning less than £20,000 a year voted 62 per cent–38 per cent to Leave.[2] The same gulf divided the big cities (78 per cent voted to Remain in several boroughs of inner London) from the outer suburbs and rural areas in England (where an average of almost two-to-one voted for Leave). And although 'too many immigrants' was one of the key messages of the Leave campaign, almost all the areas with high concentrations of immigrants voted Remain, while areas where immigrants were rarely or never seen voted strongly for Leave.

The US presidential election campaign six months later was fought on different issues and by different rules, but it is extraordinary how closely these distinctions between British Leave and Remain voters prefigure the differences between pro-Trump and anti-Trump voters in the United States in November 2016. By age, by social class, by education, and by income levels, even in terms of the urban/rural split and the dog-whistle racism and strong anti-immigrant sentiment in areas with few immigrants, American voters split in a pattern almost identical to the one seen in the United Kingdom in June 2016.[3] Indeed, even the rhetorical style of the pro-Brexit campaigners was uncannily similar to that deployed by Donald Trump, although he certainly wasn't taking any lessons from them. All this begs for an explanation, but first we need to get on with the story.

It should first be said that both sides made predictions about the future impact of Brexit on the British economy that went far beyond the available evidence. The Remain campaign persistently claimed that there would be an immediate deep recession if the country voted Leave. It is not clear if the authors of this claim really believed it, but it was dubbed 'Project Fear' by the pro-Brexit media and did indeed turn out to be untrue. In terms of outright lies, however, the Leave side definitely outdid the Remainers.

Of the Three Horsemen of the Brexit Apocalypse (the Fourth got lost along the way), Boris Johnson is closest to Trump in his relationship with the truth. He is well educated, well connected, and privileged — Eton College, Oxford University, a former mayor of London, and now Foreign Secretary — but he affects an amateurish, rather shambolic manner. He once told documentary filmmaker Michael Cockerell: 'I certainly think that as a general tactic in life, it is often useful to give the slight impression that you are deliberately pretending not to know what is going on' — and he resembles an English sheep-dog on a bad-hair day. But it is precisely this air of slightly puzzled innocence that allows him to tell barefaced lies and get away with it.

Johnson first made his name as the Brussels correspondent for the *Daily Telegraph*, one of the phalanx of right-wing British newspapers that has been spreading hatred and contempt for the EU for decades. He used to reduce his British journalistic colleagues in the European Union's capital to helpless rage by distorting or simply making up stories that portrayed the EU bureaucracy as simultaneously tyrannical and incompetent. They were usually stories about ridiculous 'Brussels red tape', such as the one about the EU banning prawn-flavoured cocktail chips.

Fifteen years ago, Johnson wrote that some of his 'most joyous hours' had been spent composing 'foam-flecked hymns of hate to the latest Euro-infamy', the banning of the prawn chips. Except, of course, that the EU didn't ban them. It merely pointed out to the United Kingdom that it had accidentally omitted prawn cocktail from a list of flavourings and sweeteners in current use in EU countries, whereupon Britain provided the information, and prawn cocktail flavouring was added to the harmonised EU-wide list.

Why was the EU keeping such a list? Because the EU 'single market' allows any member to sell its products in every other country without encountering the kind of 'non-tariff barriers' that would be created if, for example, a local producer of prawn-flavoured chips in Latvia tried to get the British product banned because it was using the wrong kind of flavouring. To prevent that sort of abuse, a list of approved products was needed. Johnson obviously knew this — he spent a long time in Brussels — but he published the story anyway. In fact, during the referendum campaign in March 2016, he told it again, citing the 'great war against the British prawn cocktail flavour crisp' as part of his evidence for Brussels-gone-mad and one of the reasons he was campaigning to leave the EU.

He told much bigger lies, too, such as the one plastered on the side of his campaign bus claiming that

Britain gave £350 million a week to the EU, money that would instead go to Britain's much-loved National Health Service if the result of the referendum was 'Leave'.

In fact, Britain gets a rebate (negotiated by Margaret Thatcher) on its contribution to the EU budget, so that it really only sends £248 million a week to Brussels. Much of that money — about £112 million a week — comes straight back to the United Kingdom in the form of subsidies for British hill-farms, British research and development, and various other worthy British causes. The net amount that Britain pays into the EU budget — much of it for infrastructure aid to poorer EU members in eastern and southern Europe — is £136 million a week. And there has never been a promise by the Conservative government to divert such a sum of money (or any other sum) to the NHS. It was pure, manipulative fantasy, but a great many people believed it. As Donald Trump once remarked (to take a quote completely out of context), 'I love the poorly educated.'

The Brexit campaign's co-leader was Michael Gove, another journalist, who was persuaded by David Cameron to leave his job as a columnist in Rupert Murdoch's UK flagship, *The Times*, and run for parliament. He ended up as education minister and then justice minister in David Cameron's cabinet. His hostility to the European Union, he claimed, had begun in his teens, when he watched his father's fishing business die under the impact of the EU's Common Fisheries Policy. (UK coastal waters are some of the richest fishing grounds on Europe's Atlantic coast, and one of the prices that Britain paid when it negotiated its entry into the organisation was to let Spanish, French, and other EU fishermen fish in those waters, too.) Gove's anger was real: in an interview on Sky News during the campaign, he described the EU as 'a job-destroying machine' run by 'sneering elites'. He served as the sober alternative for those who were put off by Boris Johnson's flamboyant upper-class-twit act, and when he denied any ambition to lead the Conservative Party, people almost believed him.

The third key figure in the Leave campaign was Nigel Farage, the founder and leader of the United Kingdom Independence Party. He began his career as a commodity trader on the London Metal Exchange, but divided his time between business and politics after the creation of UKIP in 1993, and devoted himself almost entirely to politics after his election as a member of the European Parliament in 2003. He was profoundly opposed to Britain's membership in the EU, and his anti-immigrant rhetoric won him growing support with those sections of the English public (older, whiter, non-metropolitan, and often less well educated) who were upset by the speed at which the country was changing.

It was Farage who came up with the story that 77 million Turks were about to be given the right to travel to the EU without visas, and implied that they would then all be able to settle in Britain. It was pure nonsense, of course, but it got such a strong response from the target audience in England that it was immediately taken up by Boris Johnson and the right-wing press as well. By the end of the campaign, Farage was posing

THE EU AND BREXIT: IMMIGRANTS OR JOBS? 73

in front of giant posters showing an endless queue of Syrian refugees and labelled 'Breaking Point' — as if those refugees, too, would all be coming to Britain unless the country left the EU. Given the closeness of the referendum outcome, it seems safe to say that it would have been a Remain victory if Farage, and, to a lesser extent, Johnson, had not deliberately incited a racist panic in a key section of the voting population.

So the job was done — but those who did it were astonished by their own success. Boris Johnson was a political opportunist who had only joined the Leave campaign at the last moment, presumably because he believed that an honourable failure in that endeavour would give him a better claim on the Conservative Party leadership when Cameron finally retired. He seemed terrified by his referendum victory, probably because he feared that he was about to inherit the thankless and perhaps impossible task of ending Britain's EU membership without destroying the British economy. He was very subdued on his one public appearance on the day after the referendum — which gave Michael Gove the time to stab him in the back. Having first agreed to manage Johnson's leadership bid, Gove then declared that he had realised Johnson was temperamentally unsuited to be prime minister — and presented himself as the candidate instead.

Even in the Conservative Party, this was seen as an act of treachery too flagrant to be rewarded, and Gove's leadership bid quickly collapsed. This left only Theresa May and Andrea Leadsom, the energy minister in Cameron's cabinet, in the running. Leadsom made the mistake of claiming she was the better candidate because May had never been a mother, and was quickly forced to apologise and end her candidacy. Two weeks after the referendum, Theresa May, who had never publicly supported Brexit, was prime minister. As for Nigel Farage, on 4 July he declared that his work was done, and resigned as the leader of UKIP, explaining that 'I want my life back.' The head of the Alliance of Liberals and Democrats for Europe in the European Parliament, Guy Verhofstadt, called them all (including Cameron) 'rats fleeing a sinking ship', and there was indeed a rather rodentine air to the proceedings.[4]

The possibility that empathy resides in parts of the brain so ancient that we share them with rats should give pause to anyone comparing politicians with those poor, underestimated creatures.

Frans de Waal, Charles Howard Candler Professor of Primate Behavior, Emory University, Atlanta, Georgia[5]

Brexit was not the result of long forethought and clever strategy. It was a train-wreck. The major players were making it up as they went along, and there was no planning even for the morning after, let along for the longer term. Moreover, although the economic and political consequences for the United Kingdom might be dire — the value of the British pound crashed by 10 per cent against the US dollar as soon as the referendum result became known, and ten months later the First Minister of Scotland, Nicola Sturgeon, declared that

she would seek a second independence referendum —
it seemed to be a fairly self-contained disaster.° Who,
apart from the British themselves, would be badly hurt
by the country's exit from the EU?

Yet within days, Americans were worrying aloud that
if the British could do this to themselves, Americans
might really elect Donald Trump. Maybe the underlying
circumstances that had made such a bizarre outcome
possible in the UK also existed in the United States.

It was a good question then, and the fact that Donald
Trump really did get elected makes it an even better
question now. What might the underlying circumstances
be that make these unwelcome surprises possible? The
possible answers that have been suggested include,
in no particular order, free trade and globalisation;
the widening gap between rich and poor, even in the
developed democracies; too many immigrants; the
impact of automation on jobs; the rise of social media
— or, of course, all of the above. But where do you start
looking, and how do you decide what weight to assign to
the various possible causes of the new populism?

One clue is the sheer level of anger displayed by
those who voted for Brexit, or later for Trump. There
were plenty of people who knew that the populists'

° The first Scottish referendum on independence, in 2014, resulted in a 55
per cent–45 per cent majority for staying in the United Kingdom. Sturgeon's
excuse for holding a second referendum was that Scotland had voted almost
two-to-one to stay in the EU, and that it was 'democratically unacceptable'
that it should be dragged out of the EU by non-Scottish votes. However,
after her Scottish National Party lost 21 of its 56 seats in the Westminster
parliament in the British general election of 2017, she put the idea of a
referendum on hold for at least several years.

promises were mostly lies — pro-Brexit voters who did not believe the numbers on Boris's bus for one moment, Kentucky ex-coal miners who knew that neither Donald Trump nor even the Lord Almighty on stilts could revive the US coal industry — but who were still going to vote for them. In Britain, at least, they were so angry that after the referendum it quickly became the conventional political wisdom that politicians must not hold a second referendum on the terms Britain manages to negotiate for leaving the EU, nor dilute a 'hard' Brexit by trying to stay in the customs union or the single market, lest it trigger civic unrest (that is, actual bloody riots, though they never make that explicit) by Brexit voters who feel betrayed.

It's hard to believe that the passions of millions of British voters — well, millions of English voters, to be precise — have actually been roused by abstract concepts such as the internal market. They are more likely to be angry or frightened (or both) about something else, with EU membership merely serving as a convenient symbol for all that. Which means that the Brexiteers are riding a tiger, because just taking the UK out of the EU will not assuage the anger of their supporters. They have to figure out what has really made them so angry. So do we.

Was it immigration that drove the anger? That is the answer most Tories have settled on, which is why the 'freedom of movement' rule in the EU — any citizen of an EU country can move to any other member country and live there, even set up a business there, without asking permission — became the reddest of red lines for the May government. If Britain must go on welcoming any EU citizen who wants to move there in order to retain access to the single market and a customs union with the European Union, it will just do a 'hard Brexit' and let those things go, regardless of the damage it does to the British economy. 'No deal is better than a bad deal,' as Theresa May used to repeat at frequent intervals.

Now, there are certainly quite a few immigrants in Britain: at least 3 million EU citizens, most of whom arrived from Eastern European countries in the past ten years, plus around another 5 million from the rest of the world who arrived over the past four or five decades. In a total population of 66 million, however, only 13 per cent of the people in the UK are foreign-born, which is in the same range as Germany or the United States (both 14 per cent), although significantly lower than Canada (20 per cent) or Australia (27 per cent). Of course, the ratio of foreign-born in big cities is much higher: 37 per cent in London, exactly the same as New York City. But there is nothing special about the British experience that would justify an extreme reaction against immigrants — and, in fact, there probably hasn't been one.

There is a good deal of anecdotal evidence that open racial abuse against visible minorities, foreign-born or not, has increased in the UK since the referendum, but this doesn't necessarily mean that the number of racists has grown. It is more likely to mean that some people who used to be deterred from acting their feelings out in public by a general atmosphere that was intolerant of racist abuse now feel licensed to say what they really think by the violent rhetoric of some

Brexiteers during the referendum campaign. The rise in abuse has certainly shaken the confidence of some immigrants, who have been made to feel that they are no longer welcome in the country, but it is doubtful that the situation has actually changed much at all.

The assumption in the latter stages of the referendum campaign that two-thirds of pro-Brexit voters put 'controlling' (that is, cutting) immigration ahead of any other consideration may be true, because those voters were heavily concentrated in suburban and rural parts of England where there is a kind of panic about immigration (although relatively few real live immigrants). But that is two-thirds of the 35 per cent of the population who voted Leave, not necessarily two-thirds of the entire population. Indeed, a comprehensive study carried out by the Policy Institute of King's College London, Cambridge University, and the Rand Europe think-tank in the summer of 2017 found that most people were not fixated on immigration. Nearly two-thirds of those interviewed wanted a deal that maintained close ties with the EU, and were willing to surrender a degree of sovereignty (including control over 'freedom of movement') in return for favourable trading conditions that preserved British prosperity. To the extent that they worried about immigration, most were concerned about its impact on public services, and were quite relaxed about immigrants who had jobs and paid taxes.[6]

So while immigration was an issue in the Brexit vote, it was not *the* issue. How about free trade and globalisation? This was a major theme in the US election six months later, with Donald Trump promising to renegotiate or just tear up foreign-trade agreements that allegedly destroyed American jobs, but it played a very different role in the British debate. In the Brexit battle, the question was whether British trade would be better served by membership in the EU or by an independent trade policy seeking one-off deals around the world, but nobody questioned the beneficial effect of foreign trade in general. This was doubtless related to the fact that the United Kingdom's exports amount to 27 per cent of Gross Domestic Product, while US exports only account for 14 per cent of American GDP. There has been a certain amount of 'offshoring' of British jobs over the years, but globalisation never featured prominently in the Brexit debate.

Did social media play a role? Maybe it did, but since it is mostly younger people who are heavy users of social media, and since the young voted heavily in favour of Remain, it seems probable that the net effect, if any, was pro-Remain.

The hollowing out of the middle class, and the consequent widening of the income gap between the rich and the rest, is a trend that has affected almost every developed country over the past two decades. So is the rise of automation and the consequent loss of jobs. Nor is there any doubt that these two trends are linked in various ways, although how closely remains in dispute. Could these be the real culprits of the story? As Sherlock Holmes used to say, 'Once you have eliminated the impossible, whatever remains, no matter how improbable, must be the truth.'

Actually, it's not all that improbable that unemployment and under-employment provided the essential fuel for the populist victory, for we know that the official jobless statistics are very misleading, and that British wages have stagnated or fallen in the past dozen years for all but the top 20 per cent of earners.[7] In the meantime, and before tackling the mountain of contradictions called Donald Trump, we can cheer ourselves up by examining just how deeply rooted and robust our democratic systems really are.

4

Democracy: default-mode politics

Dear Mr Willmett,
Many thanks for your letter. You ask whether totalitarianism, leader-worship etc. are really on the up-grade and instance the fact that they are not apparently growing in this country and the USA.

I must say I believe, or fear, that taking the world as a whole these things are on the increase. Hitler, no doubt, will soon disappear, but only at the expense of strengthening (a) Stalin, (b) the Anglo-American millionaires and (c) all sorts of petty fuhrers of the type of de Gaulle ... With this go the horrors of emotional nationalism and a tendency to disbelieve in the existence of objective truth because all the facts have to fit in with the words and prophecies of some infallible fuhrer. Already history has in a sense ceased to exist, ie. there is no such thing as a history of our own times which could be universally accepted ...

Private letter from George Orwell to an admirer, May 1944[1]

It was three weeks before the D-Day landings, V-1 flying bombs were landing on London every day, and George Orwell would not write *Nineteen Eighty-Four* for another three years, but his letter of May 1944 certainly has some resonance with the fears of our own time. The pessimism about the future of democracy is there, and Orwell is already worried about the 'tendency to disbelieve in the existence of objective truth'. But his vision of the future as 'a boot stamping on a human face — forever' did not come to pass, and our own worst fears about the future of democracy in an era of resurgent populism are unlikely to be fulfilled either.

This concern for the vulnerability of democracy is quite understandable, because it appeared quite late in human history and has been successfully repressed at various times and places. Because the standard historical account for the invention of democratic institutions traces only one cultural sequence, from the Greek and Roman city-states via 17th-century England and the American and French Revolutions, we also regard democracy as native to Western civilisation and transplanted (and therefore more vulnerable) elsewhere. Indeed, during the Cold War it was commonplace to see even Russia — Christian for a thousand years and a European great power for the past three hundred — as somehow outside the charmed circle of countries that had the right cultural ingredients for building a lasting democracy.

I must confess that I still held that view myself when I first went to the Soviet Union on a lengthy film shoot in 1982. It was the 'era of stagnation': most people had become privately cynical about the system, but they almost never hinted at the extent of their disaffection except to the closest and most trusted friends, and then only in the relative security of their own kitchens. In public, and especially in the company of foreigners, Soviet citizens never dared to criticise or question the Orwellian misrepresentations of reality that surrounded them, so I left the country still convinced that the communist regime, however ugly, was all-powerful and would never change. In fact, it had only seven years to go.

Five years later, after three Soviet leaders — Leonid Brezhnev, Konstantin Chernenko, and Yuri Andropov — had died in rapid succession, I went back to speak at an international conference, landed in Moscow, and realised that things really had changed under Mikhail Gorbachev. As a 'one-month expert' on Russia, I simply had not believed that all the talk of *glasnost* and *perestroika* could be genuine, but people I had known before were now speaking freely about the past, the present, and even (with some apprehension) the future.

In a couple of days, I was convinced that huge change was coming (and it felt like it might be positive change), so I decided to go back to the Soviet Union and the satellite countries for a couple of weeks every few months, get to know all the players, and interview them regularly. I didn't know it yet, but I was watching a non-violent revolution take shape in the world capital of tyranny.

Non-violent revolutions seemed like a contradiction in terms then. Mahatma Gandhi could shame exhausted imperialists into going home, and Martin Luther King could wring concessions out of elected administrations that knew they were in the wrong, no matter how furiously they denied it, but nobody had ever taken on a real dictator and forced him out of power without violence. Then, in 1986, the Filipinos did exactly that (while the whole world watched, because Manila had just got a live satellite uplink). A few other Asian countries followed their example in the next couple of years — South Korea, Thailand, and Taiwan successfully, although Burma's attempt was a bloody failure — but it still seemed inconceivable that this kind of soft power could overcome a real totalitarian autocracy. The massacre that ended the Tiananmen Square protests in Beijing in May–June 1989 just confirmed that pessimistic assessment.

So I went to the first anti-communist demonstration in Moscow the following month with grave misgivings. The rendezvous was outside the 'Stalin Gingerbread' skyscraper that housed the Ministry of Foreign Affairs. The ten-lane Garden Ring road was already jammed full of people when I got there, but I stayed close to the side of the street, not too far from a doorway of some sort, in case the shooting started. Then I realised that there were army officers in full uniform in the crowd, *and they were protesting, too* — so I got out in the middle of the street with everybody else.

I spent the rest of that summer in the Baltic republics, Ukraine and Azerbaijan, where parallel administrations run by local nationalists were already jostling the communists aside. On the way home from the Soviet

Union in September, I stopped off in Budapest — to find the streets littered with Trabant cars abandoned by East Germans who were using Hungary as an escape route to the West because the Hungarian government, though still technically communist, had opened the border with Austria. Most of the East German 'refugees' were young and well educated, and when I interviewed them in the Young Pioneer camp in the hills behind Buda where they waited for the hourly coaches to arrive and take them to West Germany, they were all confident that it wouldn't be long before the inter-German border would be open, too. As soon as I got home, I booked a flight back to Berlin, and got there just as the Wall was coming down.

What was happening was occasionally scary, but mostly it was exhilarating — and entirely counter-intuitive. It sounds almost trite now, but at the time it was a revelation to learn that people can and will act together spontaneously to resist domination, and that so long as they stay united and avoid violence, it is very hard for the 'authorities' to use violence against them. And the non-violent democratic revolutions kept coming. By the end of 1991, the Soviet Union itself had been dismantled by non-violent action (though Russia still struggles with democratisation), and the Cold War was over. Then it was the turn of apartheid South Africa, where the African National Congress never even exercised its option of flooding the streets of Johannesburg with hundreds of thousands of non-violent protesters. Had it done so, the white-minority government would have had only two choices: to surrender unconditionally without any negotiations or guarantees, or to clear the streets by gunfire and start the race war that would destroy the whole country. Instead, the ANC just held that threat in reserve while the negotiations continued for a peaceful transfer of power by means of a one-person-one-vote democratic election, which finally came in 1994.

I spent some of that year in South Africa making a film about it, but I still wasn't sure how and why non-violence worked. Clearly, it depended on media exposure to be safe: that's why it is a relatively recent phenomenon. Round-the-clock global television coverage was what emboldened the Filipinos to stand up to the dictator Ferdinand Marcos in 1986, and when the Chinese regime decided to slaughter the students on the square in 1989, believing (probably accurately) that its own political survival was at stake, it waited until after dark to send the army in so the television cameras could not record it.

Clearly, too, both the desire for equality and the instinctive knowledge that collective non-violent action will probably deter even the powerful and well-armed from resorting to violence themselves are *human* qualities, not the exclusive inheritance of some specific cultural group: Czechs and Thais and Basotho share these values and this knowledge in equal measure. If all these things didn't make you question your assumptions about the cultural roots of democracy, you really weren't paying attention.

The past is not dead. It's not even past.

William Faulkner, *Requiem for a Nun*, 1951

In all the written history of mankind, steep hierarchies of power and privilege are the default mode of human politics, with only brief outbreaks, mostly quite recent, of a different kind of politics based of egalitarian values. On the other hand, there was already wide agreement in anthropological circles that the earliest human societies, the little bands of hunter-gatherers, rarely more than a hundred in number, in which all human beings lived for several hundred thousand years, were intensely egalitarian. They had no formal leaders, no permanent hierarchies, and made their decisions by a process of discussion, debate, and consensus. So something very large must have happened five or ten thousand years ago to force almost all civilised societies into the tyrannies that fill our history — and something else very large must be happening now to allow egalitarian values to re-emerge as the political norm in contemporary mass societies.

A great many people were speculating on these questions in the late 20th century, and being a trained historian gave me no advantage at all. The answers clearly lay further back in the past, with the anthropologists, or maybe even with the primatologists, so I got in touch with Frans de Waal, whose book *Chimpanzee Politics: power and sex among apes* made a big impression on me when it was first published in 1982. He's Dutch by birth, but by 1995 he was the director of the Yerkes National Primate Research Center at Emory University in Atlanta, so I just phoned him, the way journalists do, and asked if I could come and interview him.

Not now, de Waal said: he was involved in organising a closed inter-disciplinary conference to be held at Emory. What's it about? I asked. Well, it's about the 'U-Shaped Curve', he said: the puzzling fact that most non-human primate species live in extremely hierarchical groups (a vertical line), whereas early human beings lived in remarkably egalitarian mini-societies (a horizontal line) — and civilised human beings, for the most part, have reverted to extreme hierarchies (another vertical line, and thus a U-shaped curve). The conference was closed, because all sorts of disciplines would be present, from evolutionary biologists to cultural anthropologists, and none of the participants wanted to risk their reputations by being involved in this speculation on a large new topic until they were certain that the conference had produced academically respectable results. Oh, please, can I come, I said. I promise I'll only interview people who are willing to go on the record, and I won't record or repeat anything that is said in the public sessions. And, amazingly, he let me come.

The conference went well, and some very interesting ideas were aired. Although I had no professional standing at the conference, by the end of it I could barely contain myself from pointing out that the puzzle was not just a U-shaped curve. It was more like the cross-section of a saucepan, and the (horizontal) saucepan handle was what had happened over the past two-and-a-half centuries in the West and was happening all around the planet right now: the re-emergence of egalitarian values in politics and the spread of democratic systems in modern mass societies.

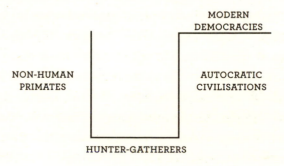

All men seek to rule, but if they cannot rule they prefer to remain equal.

Harold Schneider, economic anthropologist, 1979[2]

By my definition, egalitarian society is the product of a large, well-united coalition of subordinates who assertively deny political power to the would-be alphas in their group.

Christopher Boehm, evolutionary anthropologist, director, Jane Goodall Research Center, University of Southern California, 1999[3]

When we talk about democracy, what we really mean is a society of equals — which is pretty rare both in human history and among primates in general. But such societies did exist, probably for at least one hundred thousand years, and maybe much longer, in human *pre*history. In fact, they were almost certainly the norm.

It wasn't democracy in the modern sense, with elections and elected leaders: the little bands of hunter-gatherers could settle everything directly, just by talking things over until a consensus was reached and a decision emerged. It took a long time, because everybody had an equal right to speak, and they weren't usually in a hurry. But these were societies where all the adults were genuinely equal and there were no leaders giving orders.

Anthropologists don't have time machines, of course, so they had to make do with studying the few dozen hunter-gatherer societies that had survived into the 20th century relatively intact (although almost all of them had had some contact by then with the big civilisations that surrounded them). And the fact that they were practically all egalitarian, in polar environments and tropical ones, in deserts or forests, in every continent, emboldened the anthropologists to speculate that all the hunter-gatherer bands of the distant past — everybody's ancestors, in other words — had also been egalitarian. Or democratic, to use the modern word for the kind of politics that egalitarianism enables.

This idea was already gaining ground in anthropological circles in the late 1960s, when most people outside the trade still assumed that our distant ancestors, long before civilisation, had been nasty, brutish, and quite short. (Think of the opening scenes from Stanley Kubrick's *2001: a space odyssey*, released in 1968.) By the late 1980s, most anthropologists accepted that their hunter-gatherer ancestors had actually been quite nice to one another, at least within their own band. (They did fight wars against neighbouring bands.)

But even before the general public had caught up with the new thinking, the anthropologists were developing grave doubts about the idea that human beings might be innately egalitarian.

> The three African great apes, with whom we share this rather recent Common Ancestor, are notably hierarchical ... The same can be said of most human political societies in the world today, starting about five thousand years ago ... From certain well-developed chiefdoms came the six early civilizations, with their powerful and often despotic leaders. But before twelve thousand years ago, humans basically were egalitarian.
> Bruce Knauft, cultural anthropologist[4]

The problem for anthropologists with this business of egalitarian hunter-gatherers was the fact that all our closest relatives, the other great apes, are clearly quite nasty. Sorry, I mean hierarchical. Young male chimpanzees setting out to climb the status ladder start by beating up on adult females before they dare to take on rival young males. 'Silverback' gorillas keep harems of females; some of their young sons are allowed to remain, but not to breed. Bonobos are less violent, but both males and females live in clearly defined dominance hierarchies. And most human societies for the past five thousand years have had kings at the top and slaves at the bottom.

So the notion that 'Anatomically Modern Humans', during their two-hundred-thousand-year tenure on this planet, have lived in egalitarian societies for at least half the time, if not more, poses a problem. By the 1980s most anthropologists did believe that this was the fact of the matter — the evidence from extant hunter-gatherer bands was so strong — but it was a fact that begged for an explanation. If they were the egalitarian exception in a sea of primate despotism, how did they get there?

Maybe they became egalitarians only one hundred thousand years ago, or maybe the switch goes further back — the archaeological record gives us little direct evidence about our ancestors' social arrangements — but at some point in the distant past there must have been a revolution that overthrew the traditional primate hierarchy. And then, between five and ten thousand years ago, there must have been a counter-revolution that drove all the newly 'civilised' peoples back into steeply hierarchical societies — which 99 per cent of human beings lived in until the first democratic revolutions in America and Europe less than ten generations ago.

Anthropologists don't get involved in debates about where the modern revolutions came from, although they are well aware of the relevance of their own work for understanding that. It is the first two big changes, the egalitarian revolution and the hierarchical counter-revolution, that concern them. The first man to call a puzzle that they created the 'U-shaped curve' was Bruce Knauft, a colleague of Frans de Waal's in the anthropology department at Emory University, in an article in 1991. Two years later, Christopher Boehm of the University of Southern California published a paper in *Current Anthropology*, suggesting how egalitarian behaviour might first have arisen in human beings,[5] and by 1995 there they all were at Emory with a couple of dozen other experts in various fields to take a good long look at the evidence.[6]

The symposium didn't shake the foundations of anthropology, but it did mark a major shift in the way that anthropologists and allied trades address the political dimension of human nature. Four years later, Boehm published his book *Hierarchy in the Forest: the evolution of egalitarian behavior*, with a proposed explanation for how egalitarianism had happened in the first place, and then been suppressed again at the dawn of civilisation, that actually makes sense. It's not the last word on the subject — there's never a last word in science, and especially in the social sciences — but it's a very persuasive working hypothesis, and I will be working with it for the rest of this chapter.

Boehm's key insight is that human beings, as one of the great apes and part of the broader primate family, inevitably have a strong tendency to seek domination over their fellows: you can't escape from your own heredity. However, being more intelligent than their primate relatives, human beings can also foresee where this tendency is likely to lead, and it's nowhere good. An individual's personal chance of emerging as 'top dog' is very small: every player except one is going to lose this game. Ending up at the bottom of the pecking order is very undesirable, but much more likely. So for most people, just abolishing the pecking order and enforcing equality across the entire group you live in becomes a most attractive option. As Boehm explained:

The hypothesis was straightforward: such people are guided by a love of personal freedom. For that reason they manage to make egalitarianism happen, and do so ... in spite of innate human tendencies to dominance and submission that easily lead to the formation of social dominance hierarchies. People can arrest this process by reacting collectively, often pre-emptively, to curb individuals who show signs of wanting to dominate their fellows ... This hypothesis provided a curious answer to Knauft's riddle, for I was arguing that the same quite definite and 'hierarchical' human political nature could [support not only the] despotic societies of recent humans and ancestral apes, but also the egalitarian societies of [early] humans. In despotic social dominance hierarchies the pyramid of power [has] one or a few individuals (usually male) at the top exerting authority over a submissive rank and file. In egalitarian hierarchies the pyramid of power is turned upside down, with a politically united rank and file decisively dominating the alpha-male types.[7]

Boehm's hypothesis had the great advantage that it did not require us to re-invent humans as a species without ambition or envy in order to explain the triumph of egalitarianism. All it requires is a broad coalition of people who do not want to lose out in the dominance game — and know they are unlikely to win it — to band together and use their numbers to create a political environment in the band that deters the alpha-males from seizing control. As Harold Schneider said, 'All men seek to rule, but if they cannot rule they prefer to remain equal.'

Why did only humans, of all the primates, do this? A very clever chimpanzee might dimly apprehend this principle, but he has no language to formulate it clearly even for himself, let alone to communicate it to the other chimpanzees who are also intimidated and oppressed by the highest-ranking member of the band. Lower-status chimpanzees do engage in quite sophisticated politics, including forming coalitions to overthrow the band's current despot, but it always ends up with a new tyrant taking his place. Meet the new boss, same as the old boss. Whereas a human coalition — remember, we're only talking about a dozen or so adult men in the band, most of whom have known one another since childhood — might manage to stick together, prevent new tyrants from emerging, and shut the whole dominance game down. Boehm calls the technique by which they accomplished that a 'reverse dominance hierarchy'.

Not only might this have happened early on in human prehistory; it *must* have happened, and not once but many times. There is no other way that a primate species such as our own could have ended up living with almost perfect equality among adults in each of its tens of thousands of scattered bands for thousands of generations. We have no evidence for when this revolution happened, but it must have been long ago, for the mechanisms by which the potentially dominant members of a band are prevented from taking over are deeply embedded in the culture of almost all hunter-gatherer groups that survived long enough for anthropologists to get to them. Indeed, even most 'tribal' groups — that is, groups that have begun to domesticate plants and/or animals, live in villages of up to several hundred people that only move infrequently if at all, and may number into the thousands or even more in total — also remain egalitarian, and have the same levelling customs to ensure that no individual or group of individuals comes to dominate the rest.

This is most striking when dealing with leaders. There aren't any, in the conventionally understood sense of the word. Some individuals are more respected and influential on account of their wisdom, experience, or prowess as warriors, but they have no permanent mandate to take charge of the group and give orders, even in times of crisis. Indeed, when important decisions are taken they tend to be among the last to speak, summing up the discussion when the outlines of a consensus have already become clear. And even among the tribal peoples who stay put long enough to accumulate a certain amount of material wealth, greater generosity in sharing is expected from those who attain social prominence than from others. Indeed, the ideal characteristics of a person who might be considered for a leadership role, however temporary and conditional, would include generosity, modesty, and an even disposition, whereas a tendency to anger, arrogance, boastfulness, or even aloofness are all strongly disapproved of. As Richard Lee says of the San ('Bushman') group of hunter-gatherers in the Kalahari desert of southern Africa with whom he lived for several years: 'In !Kung terms these traits absolutely disqualify a person as a leader and may engender even stronger forms of ostracism.'

Say that a man has been hunting. He must not come home and announce like a braggart, 'I have killed a big one in the bush!' He must first sit down in silence until I or someone else comes up to his fire and asks, 'What did you see today?' He replies quietly, 'Ah, I'm no good for hunting. I saw nothing at all … maybe just a tiny one.' Then I smile to myself because I now know he has killed something big.

A proud hunter's heavy use of denial and euphemism demonstrates the degree to which the group is able to intimidate its more prominent achievers. And even after his show of modesty, other band members pre-emptively take pains to put down the hunter. When they go to carry in the kill, they express their 'disappointment' boisterously:

You mean to say you have dragged us all the way out here to make us cart home your pile of bones? Oh, if I had known it was this thin I wouldn't have come. People, to think I gave up a nice day in the shade for this. At home we may be hungry but at least we have nice cool water to drink.

The actual feelings of the critics, who simultaneously are joking and deadly serious, is revealed in the words of a culture member:

When a young man kills much meat, he comes to think of himself as a chief or a big man, and he thinks of the rest of us as his servants or inferiors. We can't accept this. We refuse one who boasts, for someday his pride will make him kill somebody. So we always speak of his meat as worthless. In this way we cool his heart and make him gentle.

A !Kung informant explaining how the social controls work[8]

Hunter-gatherer bands put an enormous amount of effort into ensuring that nobody gets too big for his boots. This includes 'randomising' the credit for major achievements that might otherwise enhance a talented individual's status and power. Killing a large animal is such an achievement, especially since the person who killed the beast then presides over the sharing out of the meat to all the heads of households in the band. (It would be unthinkable for the killer to keep all the meat for himself; big animals are always shared out more or less evenly.) The rule is that credit for the kill goes to the person whose arrow first hits the game, which seems fair enough — but that person may not even have been present on the hunt. The hunters all regularly exchange arrows, and keep track of who actually owns them. As Boehm explains: 'In effect, it is a way of removing the temptation to dominate. The fact that the best hunters speak so modestly, and frequently swap arrows to avoid envy, is a monument to the efficacy of ridicule as an instrument of social control. But as we shall see, if they are faced with serious upstartism, people like the !Kung will go far beyond ridicule.'

'Upstarts' is what Boehm calls people who challenge the egalitarian order: people whose accomplishments or just their force of personality allow them to aspire to a prominent position in the band, even to give orders to other adults (which is a shocking breach of hunter-gatherer etiquette). If the normal social controls fail to deter them, the upstarts will face ostracism, perhaps expulsion from the band, and maybe even execution. Hunter-gatherers are not sweet, gentle, ineffective people. The men amongst them are all heavily armed and proficient in the use of weapons, they have a very high murder rate, and they frequently wage war against hostile neighbouring bands. But they are dedicated to maintaining their personal autonomy, which depends on preserving their equality against all challengers and 'upstarts'. They will kill, if necessary, to 'defend the revolution' (as they would certainly not put it), but they rarely have to go so far.

We are into pure speculation here, but it is very unlikely that the 'reverse-dominance hierarchy' was imposed by killing off all the alpha types in the band. Small hunter-gatherer groups cannot afford to lose too many people, and in any case it shouldn't be necessary. From what we know now about the human dynamics of such confrontations, a united front of people demanding equality will generally overawe the despots and would-be despots. (You might even say that modern democracies are simply the way that reverse-dominance hierarchies manifest themselves in mass societies.)

The original revolution, by the way, did not include feminism. Absolute equality pertained only between the heads of households, who were generally men, and gender relations within individual families could range from equality to downright despotism. However, adult women were definitely part of the 'moral community' that maintained the egalitarian rules and judged offenders against them, and their collective power in the public domain was certainly much greater than it was in the big, intensely hierarchical societies that supplanted the hunter-gatherers starting five to ten thousand years ago.

Which brings us, of course, to the second question: why did egalitarianism collapse between five and ten thousand years ago in the Nile Valley, the Fertile Crescent, the Indus Valley, and the Yellow River Valley, and between two and three thousand years ago in Central America and the Andes as well? These were all places where agriculture was becoming more systematic and intensive, and that may have been facilitated by the warming climate (the last major glaciation ended about eleven thousand seven hundred years ago), but why would more widespread and productive farming bring the whole system of reverse dominance hierarchy crashing down? The answer is probably just numbers.

All these cradles of early civilisation saw population explosions, because food production expanded hugely. Suddenly there were groups of fifty thousand, one hundred thousand, even half a million people living in the same area. This disabled most of the social customs that kept ambitious individuals in check, since they relied on people living in small groups and knowing one another intimately. Inequality soared, too, as the domestication of oxen around 6,000 years ago enabled some farmers to plough far more land and reap far more grain than others: those who owned the oxen were the first wealthy class, and it shows in the size of their houses. At the same time, the size and complexity of these new societies created a need for strong, centralised leadership that had previously been absent. And there were, of course, lots of people who would be more than happy to act as leaders. The rest, quite literally, is history.

Men neither bought nor sold; there were no poor and no rich; there was no need to labour, because all that men required was obtained by the power of will; the chief virtue was the abandonment of all worldly desires. The Krita Yuga was without disease; there was no lessening with the years; there was no hatred or vanity, or evil thought; no sorrow, no fear.

Mahabharata, ca. 200 AD[9]

In the age when life on earth was full, no one paid any special attention to worthy men, nor did they single out the man of ability ... They loved each other and did not know that this was 'love of their neighbour.' They deceived no one, yet did not know that they were 'men to be trusted'. They were reliable and did not know that this was 'good faith.' They lived freely together, giving and taking, and did not know that they were generous.

Chuang Tzu, 369–286 BC[10]

We don't know what happened in detail, because it happened in a period before there was writing to preserve the evidence, but it seems likely that the

transition from little egalitarian societies to large
centralised monarchies with god-kings and slaves may
have taken less than a thousand years (and a great deal
of violence, of course). However, there must have been
a widespread folk nostalgia for the lost egalitarian past,
as there are myths of a lost Golden Age in all of the Old
World's dawn civilisations — the Perfect Age (Krita
Yuga) in India, the Age of Perfect Virtue in China, the
Garden of Eden in Middle Eastern cultures — even
though all of them were first written down thousands
of years after the actual change came about in their
respective societies. Chuang Tzu even writes that 'in the
Age of Perfect Virtue men lived ... on terms of equality
with all creatures, as forming one family; how could they
know among themselves the distinctions of superior
men and small men?'

Nothing remained in the material world by then to
suggest that equality had ever been a human value, but a
strong personal preference for the old egalitarian values
survived even in the new civilisations. It has been argued
that the reign of reverse dominance hierarchies lasted
long enough — one or two thousand generations — for
egalitarian values to be incorporated into the human
genetic heritage, and that is theoretically possible, but
we need not insist upon it. It suffices to point out that
midway between the rise of mass civilisations and the
present, around two millennia ago, new universalist
religions arose — Buddhism, Christianity, Islam —
that all declared the absolute spiritual equality of all
believers.

Why would we be surprised by this? In the everyday

life of ordinary human beings, functional egalitarianism never went away. Today, the average person knows about the same number of people as friends and acquaintances as they would have in a hunter-gatherer band. The big difference is that back in the prehistoric days, that would have included pretty much everybody they ever met; now, it is a smaller selection of people whom they choose to include in their personal circle of friends and acquaintances. But among these overlapping circles of friends and acquaintances, the operational assumption is and always has been a rough degree of equality. Just as hunter-gatherer societies had an egalitarian ethos but struggled constantly to suppress dominance-seeking behaviours, so the hierarchical mass societies have always had to contend with a rival set of egalitarian values held in private by their own subjects.

Nevertheless, the daily reality of the new mass civilisations was universal hierarchy, militarisation, and oppression. For most people, the agricultural revolution — or perhaps we should say counter-revolution — was a disaster. They lost their freedom, they had poorer diets, they died younger, and they were even physically stunted compared to their hunter-gatherer ancestors. But they multiplied like rabbits, and in only a few thousand years they pushed the hunter-gatherers and the tribal peoples out of all the good lands. Egalitarian values resurfaced briefly a few times in the classical period, notably in Athenian democracy and the Roman republic, but none of these experiments included more than a fraction of the local population. Ninety-nine per cent of the human race lived under kings, emperors, and dictators — and the tyrannies lasted for five thousand years, give or take a few centuries.

Then, around 1450, Johannes Gutenberg introduced the printing press and moveable type to Europe.

> We have it in our power to begin the world over again.
>
> Thomas Paine, *Common Sense*, 1776

Moveable type had been invented in China four centuries before Gutenberg, but it did not flourish in a language that used thousands of different ideographs: it was too costly to keep a set of type that contained 100,000 or more blocks, including dozens or hundreds of copies of the more common characters, so printers mostly stuck with woodblocks instead. European languages written in alphabetic scripts needed only fifty or sixty different pieces of type, and publishing immediately became a profitable and growing industry: around 10 million books were printed in Europe in the 15th century, 200 million in the 16th, and half a billion in the 17th. Tom Paine's 1776 pamphlet *Common Sense*, advocating the establishment of an independent, democratic republic in what would become the United States, sold 120,000 copies in the first three months in the Thirteen Colonies, and may have been read by half the population (then about 2.4 million).

It was no coincidence that the first modern democratic revolution happened in the Thirteen Colonies. Most of the colonists were of English descent, and were therefore heirs to the English Civil War of the

1640s and the Glorious Revolution of 1688, which had established the principle that the king ruled only with the consent of parliament. Equally importantly, about 85 per cent of men in New England could read, and although literacy was lower in the southern colonies and among women, it is probable that around half the total adult population was literate. This was even higher than in England, and indeed was probably the highest literacy rate in the world in the 1770s.

Printing and literacy mattered so much because they restored to populations numbering in the millions the ability to discuss means and ends and to come to collective decisions that had been lost with the rise of the mass civilisations. The first mass medium, the printing press, removed the roadblock that had made democracy — the political expression of the principle of equality in a mass society — virtually impossible for so long. Given the suppressed longing for equality that had never been extinguished in the mass societies, despite thousands of years of repression, people were bound to take advantage of the new circumstances to take it back.

Conducting the debate through newspapers, pamphlets, books, and large public meetings was obviously a more cumbersome and less satisfactory process than the old hunter-gatherer decision-making tradition of a few dozen adults debating decisions around a campfire until a consensus emerged, but it could be made to work. In an astonishingly short time, the mechanisms of a representative democracy were designed and put into place in the United States, including the constitutional 'checks and balances' that would serve as a modern and less oppressive substitute for the obsessive levelling customs of the hunter-gatherers. The constitution that incorporated the revived egalitarian values and the new rules and devices needed to make a mass democracy work was signed in 1787, and still works today — even though the American population has increased a hundredfold.

In 1789, thirteen years after the outbreak of the American War of Independence in 1776, the revolution reached France, at the time the biggest and most powerful country in Europe, and the avalanche really got underway. It is still not over today, but a majority of the world's people now live in countries that call themselves democratic. Quite a lot of them really are.

Good, but it's a bit early to rejoice. It probably always will be. When asked what the Constitutional Convention of 1787 had achieved, Benjamin Franklin allegedly replied: 'A republic … if you can keep it,' and that conditionality still applies today. Even the best-run, most experienced democracies still have to contain the ambitions of those who would dominate them without crushing the freedom of everybody else, and the balance is always hard to maintain.

The first two centuries of the democratic revolution were turbulent and bloody — France is now working on its fifth republic — and progress was slow. The old order defended itself ferociously, and even at the end of the First World War less than half the population of the West lived in genuinely democratic countries, and almost nobody outside the West. (Most non-Westerners, of course, lived under the heel of one European empire or another.) Moreover, the early 20th century saw the emergence of two extreme forms of politics that threatened to subvert or divert the drive for democracy.

One was fascism, which destroyed the existing hierarchies but substituted its own monolithic power structure and subordinated every member of the society to the goal of subjugating rival societies and establishing its own dominance. Chimpanzee politics writ very large, you might say. The other, communism, was a far greater challenge to the egalitarian ideal, for it simply took it to an extreme. It proposed that people should again live in the same circumstances of absolute material equality that our hunter-gatherer ancestors did (though its founders, of course, were not aware of that analogy). Marx even suggested that the state would eventually wither away, presumably leaving people to organise their lives in the same informal and consensus-seeking way that the ancestors did.

It was a sweet idea, but it failed to recognise that the degree of external political control that would be required to make people accept the goal of absolute material equality, in the absence of the kind of internalised social controls that the hunter-gatherers used, meant that communist societies had to be totalitarian tyrannies. And those tyrannies, of course, generated their own status hierarchies, and so led to levels of corruption that were significantly higher than those in capitalist societies. (But give Marx some credit: we do use 'capitalist', the word he popularised, to describe our own societies.)

The fascists were defeated in twenty years, at the

cost of the worst war in history. The communists didn't go under for another forty-odd years, during which we all lived with the threat of a far greater war that could even have triggered a 'nuclear winter', but in the end they left the stage quite peacefully. (There are still a few countries in Asia and one in Latin America that call themselves communist, but most of them seem to have lost the faith.) Apart from the Muslim world, which is fighting a string of vicious international and civil wars over the whole question of modernisation (which includes democratisation), the wars in defence of democracy are largely over, at least for the moment.

Thanks to the techniques of non-violent revolution, the past thirty years have seen a rapid spread of democracy in the post-colonial world. Despite some backsliding (in, for example, Turkey, Thailand and the Philippines) about half the world's population now lives in democratic countries. To the extent that is possible in complex and inter-connected societies that are the heirs to five thousand years of civilisation, we have got our old equality and freedom back — and we get to keep the manifold benefits of that civilisation, too.

Yes, seven billion people (heading for eleven billion) is too many. Yes, climate change. Yes, the Sixth Mass Extinction. Yes, I know that we are running very close to the wind, but given how much worse we could have screwed up, I think we are actually doing pretty well at this point.

I also know that human ingenuity is capable of subverting any institution that human beings have created, and that we have no guarantee that egalitarian values will still prevail in the latter half of the 21st century. But I don't think that a man as ignorant and self-indulgent as Donald Trump is going to destroy American democracy, let alone that populism is going to do it worldwide.

5

Trump: stop the world, I want to get off

As democracy is perfected, the office of president resembles, more and more closely, the inner soul of the people. We move toward a lofty ideal. On some great and glorious day the plain folk of the land will reach their heart's desire at last, and the White House will be adorned by a downright moron.

H.L. Mencken, 1920

Mencken will have to wait a little longer. The word 'moron' was only coined in 1912, originally as a medical term denoting an adult with a mental age of about eight to twelve. It does not apply to Donald Trump, whose cognitive skills often seem fully adult, apart from a very short attention span: ignorance is not the same as stupidity.

Trump's most startling defect is not intellectual but emotional. By the age of eight or ten, most children are already displaying a higher level of emotional maturity than the US president, and the vast majority of American adults certainly do. So how did he persuade them to elect him to the presidency, and what (if anything) does that tell us about the future of democracy in America?

The first thing to be said about Trump's election victory in November 2016 is that it was not a landslide, or even a very big change in the usual voting patterns. Hillary Clinton got almost exactly the same number of votes in 2016 as Barack Obama got in 2012, and Donald Trump only got 2 million more than Mitt Romney did in 2012. Most people, clearly, were voting for the same party they always voted for, even if some of them were holding their noses: party played a bigger role than personality. And the Democratic candidate led the Republican in the popular vote in both elections, although Clinton's lead (2.9 million) was just over half the size of Obama's (5 million).

Trump won in the Electoral College (which is what really counts) by taking only three key states from the Democrats, all in the Rust Belt and all by extremely narrow margins: Michigan by 10,704 votes, Wisconsin by 31,006, and Pennsylvania by 67,416. No big deal: that's how the electoral system works. But here's a significant fact: in all three states, Bernie Sanders won more than half a million votes in the Democratic primary. A very large post-election poll revealed that 12 per cent of those who voted for Sanders in the Democratic primaries then voted for Donald Trump in the presidential election.[1] They probably provided Trump's margin of victory in all three key states.

We can safely assume that it was not racism or sexism that attracted them to Sanders. According to the poll data, it was not his opposition to free trade, either. All those factors may have contributed to Trump's victory, but it wasn't what ultimately sent these voters in his direction. What Sanders and Trump did have in common was an anti-establishment stance and an explicit commitment to deal with the widening income gap between the rich and the rest. Maybe Trump was lying about his intentions, but it was definitely a big part of both men's sales pitch. So there's one clue: it's really about the economy, stupid — and especially about the growing inequalities in the economy.

The most telling statistics from the 2016 election are these. Hillary Clinton still won a narrow majority (between 51 and 53 per cent of the vote) among Americans earning less than $50,000 a year — but there was actually a 16-point net swing to the Republicans among those voters earning less than $30,000 a year, and a 6-point swing among those earning between $30,000 and $50,000 a year. (Clinton, on the other hand, benefited from a swing to the Democrats among those earning over $50,000 a year, and especially among those earning $100,000-plus.)[2] Large numbers of working-class, habitually Democratic voters who had backed Barack Obama in 2008 and 2012, presumably believing that he would do something to restore their severely eroded earnings, seem to have decided by 2016 that the Democrats were hopeless and that Trump was more likely to help them than Clinton.

However, we are so far dealing in policy proposals as

if Trump were an ordinary candidate, and he manifestly wasn't. He is a serial liar: *Toronto Star* journalist Daniel Dale tracked his rallies from 15 September to 8 November 2016, and recorded 560 false statements, an average of about twenty a day.[3] During the election campaign, he repeatedly demanded that his opponent, Hillary Clinton, be jailed ('Lock her up!'), he claimed that the election was being rigged against him, and he spouted casual racism, misogyny, and anti-Semitism. He has filed for bankruptcy six times on various of his businesses (though that's not uncommon in the property-development trade, and especially in the casino business), and he has refused to reveal his tax returns (unprecedented for forty years for a major-party presidential candidate). He is vulgar and vain, and so narcissistic that his staff have discovered that the only way to get him to read all the way through a proposal or briefing paper is to insert his name into every paragraph. In fact, he is, in the words of Tony Schwartz, the man who ghost-wrote *The Art of the Deal*, the book that first brought Trump into the public eye, 'a sociopath':

> It's been horrifying. In the nearly 30 years since the book was published, the main thing I felt was 'I want to be as far away from this man as I can', but I didn't feel I created Frankenstein, because he was a real estate developer and reality television star. Who cares? It wasn't that consequential to the world.
>
> I simply didn't think that much about it until he decided to run for president and it became clear that this wasn't going to just fade away, that he was

actually in a position to win the nomination. That's when I thought, 'Oh my God, I've contributed to creating the public image of the man who is psychopathic and people don't realise it.' ... He doesn't have any core beliefs beyond his own aggrandisement and power.

Tony Schwartz, interview with *The Observer*, 16 October 2016

Schwartz is so guilt-stricken by his actions that he fears the Trump presidency could lead to martial law, the end of press freedom, and the risk of nuclear war, but there is an alternative way to view Donald Trump. People are rightly reluctant to compare him to Hitler. (Godwin's law: the first person to mention Hitler or the Nazis in an internet debate automatically loses the argument.) Even comparisons with Benito Mussolini seem extreme, although Trump's body language, his bombast, and above all his chin are reminiscent of the Italian fascist dictator. A less alarming hypothesis is that he's the American Silvio Berlusconi.

The former Italian prime minister, who dominated that country's politics for twenty years, was a businessman with a lot of legal problems — falsified tax returns, accounting irregularities, secret offshore companies — but he owned three of Italy's six pre-cable television channels. It is widely believed that he originally sought political office mainly to make himself exempt from legal charges, and the product he was selling was simply himself. Unlike Trump, he did not hijack an existing political party; he just created his own,

Forza Italia! (Go for it, Italy!) — but he then treated its members with the same contempt that Trump shows for old-school Republicans. Nevertheless, a large section of the public loved Berlusconi for his (often deliberate) 'gaffes', including frequent sexist, homophobic, and racist comments. And after the fact, like Trump, he often denied that he had made the comments at all, blaming a 'hostile media'.

Like Trump, Berlusconi got his start in business as a property developer, although, unlike The Donald, he was not born into a rich family. He is far richer than Trump, but his political style was identical. He promised the world to the voters, with no idea how to deliver it and probably no intention to. He created a set of enemies whom he blamed for all his problems and setbacks — the media, the courts, the left, even politics as a whole — and presented himself as a plain-speaking, anti-establishment outsider who was a victim of 'political correctness gone mad'. If he lost an election or looked like he was going to lose it, he started claiming fraud and ballot-box stuffing. And, like Trump, he really admired Russia's Vladimir Putin. His prime ministerial career (four times in office) finally ended when he was convicted of tax fraud in 2013, and he would have gone to jail for four years if his age (over 75) had not allowed him to commute that to four hours a week of social service at an old people's home.

If Trump is just another Berlusconi, the United States is in trouble, but not terminal trouble. Like Berlusconi, he has no credible economic strategy and hardly any discernible political strategy beyond self-promotion, so the American economy is unlikely to do any better under his stewardship than Italy's did under Berlusconi. He is erratic and self-obsessed, but Berlusconi did not declare martial law, end press freedom, or start a war, and maybe Trump won't either. On the other hand, he could be around politically for a long time because, like Berlusconi, he has discovered just the right way to appeal to a large and deeply disgruntled section of the electorate. But we cannot entirely dismiss the Mussolini hypothesis either.

Trump may be a disgrace as a human being, but the vast majority of the people who voted for him are not. So how on Earth did a man so spectacularly unqualified to hold the highest office in a democracy nearing its 250th anniversary gain the trust of so many decent people?

He's playing you guys like a fiddle — the press — by saying outrageous things, and garnering attention. That's his strategy — to dominate the news.
    Republican candidate Jeb Bush, 29 November 2015

It may not be good for America, but it's damn good for CBS … The money's rolling in and this is fun. I've never seen anything like this, and this going to be a very good year for us. Sorry. It's a terrible thing to say. But bring it on, Donald. Keep going.
    Les Moonves, chair of CBS television, 29 February 2016[4]

Donald Trump received $5.6 billion in free 'earned' media coverage (not paid for, but 'earned' by making himself newsworthy) during the whole of his presidential campaign. This was more free coverage than was earned by Hillary Clinton, Bernie Sanders, Ted Cruz, and Marco Rubio combined.[5] The more outrageous Trump's remarks were, the more media attention he got. Since he boasted about it at the time, we can assume that this was a conscious strategy, so there is room for considerable doubt about how much he believes what he says. But he does say some remarkable things.

It is customary, and for some people extremely satisfying, to dwell upon Trump's more bizarre comments and to treasure them as proof of how vile and stupid he is. That is not the task I am engaged upon here, but it will do no harm to make these readers happy by providing a short list of the most egregious ones. Think of it as an aide-memoire.

16 June 2015 — 'They're bringing drugs. They're bringing crime. They're rapists. And some, I assume, are good people.' Trump on Mexican immigrants.

18 July 2015 — 'He's not a war hero. He's a war hero because he was captured. I like people who weren't captured.' About Senator John McCain, who was shot down over Vietnam and tortured during his six years as a prisoner-of-war.

7 August 2015 — 'You could see there was blood coming out of her eyes. Blood coming out of her wherever.' About CNN host Megyn Kelly.

9 September 2015 — 'Look at her face, would anyone vote for that?' About Carly Fiorina, one of his rivals in the Republican primaries. (A majority of white American women voted for Trump.)

21 November 2015 — 'I watched when the World Trade Center came tumbling down. And I watched in Jersey City, where thousands and thousands of people were cheering as that building was coming down.' On his baseless accusation that American Muslims celebrated the 9/11 attacks.

23 November 2015 — 'Whites killed by whites — 16 per cent, Whites killed by blacks — 82 per cent.' Image tweeted by Trump. The true figures are: Whites killed by whites — 82 per cent. Whites killed by blacks — 15 per cent.

3 December 2015 — 'I'm a negotiator like you folks … Is there anybody in this room that doesn't negotiate deals? Probably more than any room I've ever spoken.' On Jews as money-grubbing merchants — Trump to Republican Jewish Coalition board members.

18 December 2015 — 'At least he's a leader. You know, unlike what we have in this country.' On Vladimir Putin.

23 January 2016 — 'I could stand in the middle of Fifth Avenue, shoot somebody, and I wouldn't lose any voters.' On the devotion of his supporters.

6 February 2016 — 'I would bring back a hell of a lot worse than waterboarding.' On torture.

3 March 2016 — 'I guarantee you, there's no problem.' On the size of his penis.

30 March 2016 — 'There has to be some form of punishment.' On what should happen to women who have abortions if a future conservative-dominated Supreme Court outlaws them. (A majority of white American women still voted for him.)

17 April 2016 — 'If Hillary Clinton can't satisfy her husband, what makes her think she can satisfy America?' Trump re-tweet of a tweet by a supporter.

13 June 2016 — 'I called for a ban [on Muslims] after the San Bernardino attack, and was met with great scorn and anger. But now many are saying that I was right to do so.' After the attack on a gay nightclub in Orlando by an Afghan-American.

9 August 2016 — 'If she gets to pick her [Supreme Court] judges, nothing you can do, folks. Although the Second Amendment people, maybe there is, I don't know.' On the likelihood of Hillary Clinton being assassinated by anti-gun control fanatics if she wins the presidency and nominates pro-gun control judges to the Supreme Court.

10 August 2016 — 'He's the founder of Isis, OK? He's the founder. He founded Isis and I would say the co-founder would be crooked Hillary Clinton.' On Barack Obama.

7 October 2016 — 'I've gotta use some Tic Tacs, just in case I start kissing her. You know, I'm automatically attracted to beautiful — I just start kissing them. It's like a magnet. Just kiss. I don't even wait. And when you're a star, they let you do it. You can do anything. Grab them by the pussy. You can do anything.' Trump speaking to Billy Bush in the Access Hollywood tape released by the *Washington Post*.

16 October 2016 — 'The election is absolutely being rigged by the dishonest and distorted media pushing Hillary Clinton — but also at many polling places — SAD.' Trump's poll numbers were falling at this point.

Okay, that's enough. Have a quick shower, and let's get back to the business at hand. How did this character persuade 62 million Americans to vote for him?

Start with this fact: only 15 per cent of the additional wealth that the US economy has generated since the late 1970s has gone to the workers. The other 85 per cent has boosted corporate income, so the gap between rich Americans and other Americans has widened substantially. Top executives make more in the United States than in other developed countries, but the American middle class is not keeping up. Median income in Canada, traditionally 10–20 per cent below the US figure, caught up with the US median income in 2010. Incomes in northern European countries such as the Netherlands, Sweden, and the United Kingdom still trail slightly, but the gap is much less than it was even ten years ago. As for the poor, an American family at the 20th percentile of income distribution now makes much less money than a Canadian, Dutch, or Scandinavian family at the same percentile; forty years ago the reverse was true.[6]

There has been a massive shift in income distribution in the United States in the past thirty-five years. In the great post-Second World War boom between 1945 and 1980, the bottom 90 per cent of the US population received a steady 66 per cent of national income, and the growth model was a 'virtuous circle', as US economist Thomas Palley put it: '[P]roductivity growth ... drove ... wage growth, [which] fueled demand growth, which created full employment. Full employment then spurred investment, which increased productivity and supported further wage growth.'[7] The top 10 per cent of the American population did very well, too, but they only took 33 per cent of the national income.

Those decades were not some lost American golden age of prosperity, tranquillity, and universal amity: they included the Korean War, the Cuban missile crisis, the Kennedy assassination, the Vietnam War, black uprisings in US cities, and the forced resignation of president Richard Nixon. But this was when car ownership in the United States went from one per five people in 1947 to one for every two people by 1980 because working-class jobs paid real money. (The population was growing, too, so car registrations quadrupled.)[8] You may deplore the environmental damage done by all those cars, or indeed the sheer materialist greed of the whole process, but that kind of growth in consumption was seen as success by most people at the time, so they were pleased with the outcome.

And then the economic model changed.

> Practical men who believe themselves to be quite exempt from any intellectual influence are usually the slaves of some defunct economist.
>
> John Maynard Keynes, *The General Theory of Employment, Interest and Money*, 1936

It was probably the major burst of inflation in the 1970s that gave the disciples of British economist Friedrich Hayek and American economist Milton Friedman (neither of them at all defunct) their chance to promote an alternative model to the Keynesian doctrines that had dominated the long boom. The doctrine they espoused was of particular interest to practical men, because it justified behaviour that would maximise their share of the economic pie, for the 'neo-liberal' model that took over during the Reagan expansion of the 1980s included four key policies. The goal of economic management henceforward would be controlling inflation, not maintaining full employment. Globalisation of the flows of capital, trade, and people was to be encouraged. Payments to shareholders should have priority over reinvestment in the business. And trade union power should be broken in order to allow more flexible 'hire and fire' labour markets. The benefits of these policies would allegedly be higher investment rates, higher productivity, higher growth rates, higher incomes for the rich, and an eventual trickle-down of wealth to the poor. The policies were duly implemented, but only one of those benefits actually arrived: higher incomes for the rich.

Investment rates did not rise. Relative to profits, they fell. Until the 1980s, dividend payments and share buybacks accounted for only 2 per cent of American Gross Domestic Product, while profits reinvested in growing businesses through expansion or new technologies accounted for about 4 per cent: twice as much. Now it is precisely the other way around: dividends and buybacks amount to 4 per cent of GDP, and investment to only 2 per cent.[9]

Probably as a result of this fall in investment, productivity growth also slowed. The Economic Policy Institute has calculated that during the thirty-one years between 1948 and 1979, non-farm labour productivity rose by 108.1 per cent. In the following thirty-four years, 1979–2013, under the new economic model, productivity grew by only 64.9 per cent.[10] That's a pretty impressive failure, but it pales by comparison to what happened to working-class incomes.

In the Good Old Days of 1948–1979, the incomes of 'production/non-supervisory workers' (as the US Census Bureau calls them) closely tracked the growth of productivity, growing by 93.4 per cent in constant dollars over the whole period. In those days, a rising tide lifted all boats. But in 1979–2013, under the Hayek–Friedman economic model inaugurated by president Ronald Reagan, working-class incomes became completely detached from productivity. Hourly-paid workers' wages rose by only 8.6 per cent over the whole thirty-four years, while productivity grew eight times as fast. Somebody else reaped the rest of the benefit.[11]

Calculations of this sort are notoriously various and controversial, but George Monbiot, working with data gathered by the *New York Times*, came up with very similar estimates. According to Monbiot, between 1947 and 1979, US productivity rose by 119 per cent, while the income of the bottom fifth of the population (as defined by income level) rose by 122 per cent. Not bad. Whereas in the 'trickle-down period' of 1979–2009, he estimates productivity growth at 80 per cent — and observes that the incomes of the bottom fifth actually fell by 4 per cent.[12] Yet another study observes that if median American household income had kept pace with productivity increases in the last forty years, as it did in the earlier period, it would now be $92,000 a year, rather than less than $50,000.[13]

And for what it's worth, the trickle-down model also hurt US economic growth overall, down from an average of 3.8 per cent annually in the 1946–1979 period to only 2.7 per cent a year in 1981–2016.[14] But it worked wonders for those at the top of the heap.

The share of national income going to the richest 1 per cent of Americans has doubled in the past thirty years to reach 20 per cent, a level last seen in the 1880s and 1890s, the so-called Gilded Age. America's Gini coefficient, a widely used international measure of income inequality, is now the highest of any developed country.[15] And a major factor in driving working-class incomes down (and destroying some jobs entirely) was free trade.

It was very unpopular to say this at the time. 'Liberals, social democrats and moderate conservatives are on the same side in the great battles against religious fanatics, obscurantists, extreme environmentalists, fascists, Marxists and, of course, contemporary anti-globalisers,' wrote *Financial Times* columnist and former World Bank economist Martin Wolf in his book *Why Globalisation Works* (2004). Globalisation probably would have worked reasonably well if all the countries in the world had been at more or less the same level of development, with roughly similar wage costs, but of course they weren't. There were rich countries with relatively high wages (and high living costs, too), and many more poor countries where $3 a day would be regarded as a living wage.

The supporters of free trade, who at one time included almost the entire commentariat, argued that it offered these poor countries the opportunity to bootstrap themselves into the global middle class by exporting their products to the formerly closed markets of the rich countries, and it did work that way for China and a few countries in South-East Asia. They denied that the competition of these low-wage economies would drive down the incomes of working-class people in Western countries, but of course it did. For some of the larger companies in the West, it was an opportunity to reduce their costs by moving jobs abroad, or threatening to do so if the workers did not accept wage cuts. It's not possible to quantify how much of the decline in middle- and working-class American incomes in the past thirty-five years was due to globalisation, because there were a number of other factors operating as well, but the victims certainly saw free trade as a large part of the problem, and that eventually had major political consequences.

There is a moral aspect to the trade debate, because trade with the richer countries really is one of the few ways that poor countries can work their way out of poverty, but the alternative to untrammelled free trade on the model dictated by free-market radicals is not no trade at all. It is trade done in a more selective way, with due concern for domestic interests that may be gored by bad choices — or compensation for those who are being gored, if you really want to do that deal. In other words, international trade as it was conducted under the General Agreement on Trade and Tariffs (GATT) from 1947 to 1994. It consisted of lengthy rounds of international negotiation — seven in all — after which large numbers of specific tariffs were reduced or removed, if all the parties agreed. There was plenty of room for countries to opt out — and few instances where domestic wage rates took a major hit from an international trade deal. 'GATT's purpose was never to maximise free trade,' wrote economist Dani Rodrik in 2010. 'It was to achieve the maximum amount of trade compatible with different nations doing their own thing. In that respect the institution proved spectacularly successful.'[16] Indeed it was: international trade grew at 7 per cent a year for over forty years under GATT, compared to about half that in the years since it was renamed the World Trade Organization and taken over by the free-marketeers.

It should be noted at this point that practically nobody supporting the neo-liberal economic project, from Hayek and Friedman down to the humblest aspiring millionaire, ever said to themselves: *These policies will screw most of the population, and especially the poor, but who cares? They will make me richer.* Or at least they never said it, or even thought it, in exactly those words. What happens in practice is that various not-yet-defunct economists lay out their wares, as they are supposed to do, offering analyses and prescriptions that are shaped by their intellects but also by their values and experiences. Then along come the customers (the public), and they choose the ideas that resonate most strongly with *their* values, experiences, and ambitions. So people who are poor or care a lot about the poor gravitate to Keynes, and people who are rich and care less about the poor are drawn to Hayek and Friedman. Self-interest is served, but not quite consciously in most cases.

Admirers of Ayn Rand can claim an exemption on the grounds that they are fully conscious of the implications of their choice, but for most neo-liberals the choice is wrapped in fictions such as the 'iron laws of economics' and rationalisations that suggest all this is really good for the poor. 'We don't want to turn the safety net [of the welfare state] into a hammock that lulls able-bodied people into lives of dependency and complacency,' explained former Republican vice-presidential candidate and current Speaker of the House of Representatives, Paul Ryan, in 2013. 'That drains them of their will and their incentive to make the most of their lives.' Give them enough food stamps to see them through the whole month, and they'll just lie around playing online games. Hunger (in modest doses) is the spur that will save them.

As time passed and evidence accumulated that income growth had stalled for the majority of Americans, and that many were down-shifting to minimum-wage jobs or falling out of the work-force entirely, it became harder to ignore the fact that the neo-liberal project was not working as promised. But it was still working for the well off and the rich, so one presumes that the more self-aware among them just hoped the poor wouldn't notice. But they did, of course.

> You go into these small towns in Pennsylvania and, like a lot of small towns in the Midwest, the jobs have been gone now for 25 years and nothing's replaced them. And it's not surprising then they get bitter, they cling to guns or religion or antipathy to people who aren't like them or anti-immigrant sentiment or anti-trade sentiment as a way to explain their frustrations.[17]
>
> Barack Obama as a candidate for the Democratic presidential nomination, April 2008

Obama said that at a private fund-raiser in San Francisco, and he paid a high price in adverse publicity when his remarks were made public. What he said was quite true, but he didn't get the votes of those small-town Pennsylvanians because he never really confronted the neo-liberal experiment head-on. Obama inherited the crash of 2008, and as president he saved the banks and the automobile industry from bankruptcy (much thanks he got from neo-liberal Republicans for his trouble), but he seemed not to grasp that these periodic asset bubbles and crashes were happening because wage growth had been stifled. The rich had much more money than before, but tended to put it into assets rather than consumption, so the only possible source of increased demand in the economy was debt: keep the interest rates at rock-bottom, and encourage everybody to borrow for increased consumption.

Obama, like Bill Clinton before him and Tony Blair in Britain, was a 'triangulator' who tried to steer a course (or a 'Third Way', as Blair put it) between the demands of neo-liberal doctrine and the needs of his own voters — but none of these sort-of-left-wing leaders questioned the doctrine itself. They had accepted that you could only push this equality thing so far before the rich rebelled, and used their vast political and media resources to shout it down. The best they could hope for was the halfway houses of democracies with huge practical differences of income and privilege that most of us live in today.

They were right in principle. The failed communist experiments had convinced most people that the social, political, and human cost of trying to make old-style absolute equality work is just too high. We'll have to settle for what you might call 'managed inequality'. That is politically viable because human beings in large modern democracies are more tolerant of inequality than hunter-gatherers: their basic needs are covered, they tend to associate mostly with people of the same economic and social status, and the reality of considerable economic inequality in the broader society is softened by the agreeable fiction of 'equality of opportunity'. That is manifestly a fiction, however, and if the gulf between the rich and the rest gets too wide, the patience of the majority may run out. As you would expect if you know human beings, the breaking point is defined not by absolute levels of wealth but by disparities of wealth, and the patience ran out in 2016.

The people whom Obama so vividly described in his Pennsylvania comments quite rightly identified Hillary Clinton as the incarnation of neo-liberalism (even if they did not use that word). She pushed free-trade deals, she hobnobbed with bankers, she was part of the 'establishment' that exploited them, lied to them, and secretly despised them. They knew she saw them as irredeemable: 'You could put half of Trump's supporters into what I call the basket of deplorables … The racist, sexist, homophobic, xenophobic, Islamophobic — you name it. And unfortunately there are people like that. And he has lifted them up,' she said in New York two months before the election.[18] You couldn't have paid them to vote for her, although they might have voted for Bernie Sanders. And they would have voted for Donald Trump, no matter which party he was running for.

Donald Trump has been all over the political map in his long career, but from 2001 to 2008 he identified as a Democrat, and as late as 2010 more of his political donations went to Democrats than to Republicans.[19] If he had chosen to run for the Democratic presidential nomination in 2008, he would certainly have had the support of most of those small-town Pennsylvanians and people like them all over the country. It is conceivable that he could have beaten Obama to the nomination, although many in the Democratic Party would have been appalled. But then, many Republicans were appalled when Trump won the presidential nomination for their party eight years later. It made no difference. And if he had won the Democratic nomination, it is entirely possible that he could have won the 2008 election.

Donald Trump is neither a Republican nor a Democrat. He is the populist voice of the disappointed and frustrated 'angry white men' of both sexes in the United States. He said so himself in his speech accepting the Republican presidential nomination: 'I am your voice.' By themselves they were not numerous enough to give him political victory, but he could have taken over either of America's main political parties and combined its habitual supporters with his own devoted followers to win the presidency.

I do think that when you combine that demographic change [white people ceasing to be an absolute majority of the American population] with all the economic stresses that people have been going through because of the financial crisis, because of technology, because of globalization, the fact that wages and incomes have been flatlining for some time, and that particularly blue-collar men have had a lot of trouble in this new economy, where they are no longer getting the same bargain that they got when they were going to a factory and able to support their families on a single paycheck — you combine those things, and it means that there is going to be potential anger, frustration, fear. Some of it justified, but just misdirected. I think somebody like Mr. Trump is taking advantage of that. That's what he's exploiting during the course of his campaign.

President Barack Obama, 21 December 2015[20]

Every beaten-down, nameless, forgotten working stiff who used to be part of what was called the middle class loves Trump. He is the Molotov cocktail they have been waiting for, the human hand grenade they can legally throw into the system that stole their lives from them ... Trump's election is going to be the biggest 'fuck you' ever recorded in human history.

Michael Moore, 10 November 2016[21]

But as Michael Moore also remarked, it is not wise to use the vote as an anger-management tool.

Donald Trump is in the White House for four years, or maybe for eight. That is not to be excluded: the vehemence and near-unanimity with which the mainstream American media denounce him just proves to his core supporters that he is their champion against the 'establishment'. What we do not yet know (and probably he doesn't either) is whether he will turn out to be a Berlusconi or a Mussolini.

Conventional wisdom says that Trump cannot defy the US constitution and assume supreme power himself. The constitution is too strong and too deeply embedded in American consciousness for Trump to trample on the division of powers and get away with it, although he is clearly impatient with the restrictions it places on him. Congress, including even Republican senators and representatives, would resist strongly, the courts would condemn his actions, and the majority of the public would remember its democratic ideals and refuse to accept it.

On the other hand, Trump's ambition is boundless (if rather unfocussed), and his narcissism is such that he would not be daunted by the prospect of supreme power: 'I alone will solve (the terrorist problem) — and fast!,' he tweeted after the Brussels attacks in March 2016. Three months later, he said, 'I alone can fix it' (about the whole system this time) at the Republican National Convention. This is not a man who doubts his abilities — and Executive Directive 51 is still in effect. This 'homeland security–national security presidential directive', posted on the White House website by George W. Bush's administration without comment on 9 May 2007, claims that the president has the right to declare a 'catastrophic emergency', but does not specify who has the power to decide that it is over.

It defines a 'catastrophic emergency' as 'any incident, regardless of location, that results in extraordinary levels of mass casualties, damage or disruption severely affecting the U.S. population, infrastructure, environment, economy or government functions'. For the duration of the emergency, the president or his appointee would 'coordinate' the efforts of the executive branch with those of the legislative and judicial branches through a 'Continuity Policy Coordination Committee'. This appears to centralise power in the president's hands, although there are a number of classified 'annexes' that may constrain this. The directive was obviously written to deal with some extreme contingency such as a terrorist nuclear attack that wiped out much of the senior leadership of the US government, at a time when there were exaggerated fears of such an event, but the definition of a 'catastrophic emergency' is very broad, and is left to interpretation by the president.[22]

But why would President Trump want to take over everything? In the normal course of events he probably wouldn't. Trump enjoys power, but he doesn't enjoy the work that goes with it: 'I thought being president would be easier than my old life,' he lamented after a few months in the White House. But he could face demands for impeachment if the investigation into alleged collusion between the Trump campaign and the Russian government finds a smoking gun, and there is a significant possibility that senior Republicans might then pressure him to resign. (They would really much prefer to have Vice-President Mike Pence, a bona fide Republican, in the presidency.) Which way Trump would jump in that event is hard to predict.

It is also hard to predict what the popular reaction would be if an attempted Trump takeover was presented as a necessary but temporary suspension of normal freedoms to cope with some great threat or emergency. (This is the way that constitutional coups are normally justified in less fortunate countries.) Americans like to see themselves as the freedom-loving people *par excellence*, but the reality is rather more complex.

The World Values Survey of 2011 bluntly asked Americans if they approved of 'having a strong leader who doesn't have to bother with Congress or elections' — and 34 per cent agreed that that was a good idea. Among those who had only a high school education, 42 per cent agreed. If you take these answers at face value, one-third of Americans would prefer a dictatorship to democracy.[23] That is probably not an accurate representation of what Americans think at the moment, but it is generally agreed in the relevant academic circles that people's authoritarian tendencies become more intense when the familiar social order is disrupted, or when there is an external threat to their welfare. The traditional social order has been well and truly disrupted in the United States in the past several decades, not only in economic terms but also in terms of the formerly high status of whites, and especially straight, white working-class males. And terrorism, while of little importance in reality, is regularly portrayed by the media as an existential threat.

There could be considerable support for Trump as a strongman, if he played his cards right. If this conclusion seems to conflict with the previous examination of our human heritage as the descendants of egalitarian hunter-gatherers, bear in mind that democracy is really the political expression of egalitarian values. If a society becomes too unequal, democracy is not working, and people may seek their equality elsewhere. As Alexis de Tocqueville observed some time ago, 'Americans are so enamoured of equality that they would rather be equal in slavery than unequal in freedom.'

If this entire discussion seems a trifle far-fetched, however, that is because it is. Donald Trump's character is not the stuff of which dictators are made — unless, of course, he is secretly a highly disciplined person with a strong and clear political vision, cleverly hiding behind a facade of ignorance and fecklessness until his rendezvous with destiny finally arrives. That seems unlikely. He is much more likely to be a Berlusconi: what you see is what you get. In that case, the United States is in for a prolonged period of misgovernment, and none of the trends in politics and the economy that have delivered the country into this sorry state will be reversed in the near future. Indeed, they will probably get worse. But it takes a long time to ruin a country irretrievably, and there will be electoral opportunities to shorten the ordeal every two years.

What will be important after Trump is for the government to start rectifying the huge inequalities and the consequent disaffection of so many Americans that made his victory possible, and to do it very fast lest even worse befall the nation in another electoral cycle or two. This requires a clear understanding of how it all went wrong.

Is the neo-liberal order still the main problem, or is that already in decline? Is globalisation a real threat, or just a red herring? And how on Earth are we going to cope with automation when it really takes over?

6

Globalisation or automation: what killed the jobs?

[Globalization] has lifted more people out of poverty around the world than probably any other advance in recent history. It has certainly helped expand our prosperity here at home ... So there is no escaping this, and what we have to do in America today is figure out how to best harness the force of globalization to ensure a continuing quality of life and standard of living.

Hillary Clinton, speech in Silicon Valley, 1 May 2016

Surprise, surprise. Workers in Britain, many of whom have seen a decline in their standard of living while the very rich in their country have become much richer, have turned their backs on the European Union and a globalized economy that is failing them and their children ... That increasingly globalized economy, established and maintained by the world's economic elite, is failing people everywhere ... We need to fundamentally reject our 'free trade' policies and move to fair trade.

> Bernie Sanders, *New York Times*, 27 June 2016

Globalization has made the financial elite who donate to politicians very, very wealthy ... But it has left millions of our workers with nothing but poverty and heartache.

> Donald Trump, speech in Monessen, Pennsylvania, 28 June 2016

Hillary Clinton was trimming her sails by midway through the 2016 election campaign, because her views on free trade were clearly not playing well with many traditionally Democratic voters, but she could neither abandon her fundamental faith in globalisation nor deny her long connection with the policy. (It was her husband, Bill, who signed the North American Free Trade Agreement in 1993, although it was negotiated by his predecessor, Republican president George H.W. Bush.)

Bernie Sanders, who gave Mrs Clinton a good run for the presidential nomination, had figured out long before that many if not most Democratic voters were looking for a better answer to their economic plight than more of the same. He was dead wrong about Britain, where globalisation barely got mentioned in the Brexit campaign, but his rhetoric resonated strongly with Americans who were sick of being told how wonderful globalisation was while their own incomes stagnated and 'blue-collar' jobs disappeared. Trump was saying the same thing but in a punchier way, with promises of a wall on the Mexican border and a 45 per cent tariff on imports from China.

It's hardly surprising that globalisation got so much emphasis in the US election, because both of the competing explanations for what had gone wrong were off-limits for at least two of the leading three contenders. None of them wanted to talk about automation, because if you have no plausible solution to a problem, it's safer not to bring it up at all. Clinton and Trump were also uncomfortable condemning the neo-liberal ideology that both of their parties had espoused unquestioningly for at least a quarter-century: Sanders, as a self-declared 'democratic socialist', was the only one willing to talk explicitly about the damage that neo-liberalism has inflicted on working-class living standards. By default, therefore, globalisation became the alleged prime culprit for the profound unhappiness and disaffection of the 'white working class'. That was bound to favour a Trump victory — and when Trump says 'globalisation', he mainly means free trade.

I discussed the role of free trade in driving down American wages in the previous chapter. Here I look at it as an actual killer of jobs, and that is a different question. Was there a tidal wave of cheap imports that drove American companies making the same goods out of business? This certainly did happen in the 1970s and 1980, particularly to the American textile industry: only exclusive branded clothing is now made in the United States, and not much of that. The other 98 per cent of the clothes that Americans wear are made abroad. But the direct impact of free trade on American jobs has been quite limited, because the United States is the least trade-dependent of all the developed economies.

In 2015, trade accounted for only 27 per cent of US Gross Domestic Product, compared with an average of 56 per cent for all OECD countries and 84 per cent for the German economy.[1] More than in any other developed country, the American economy is driven primarily by domestic factors, with imports and exports playing a relatively minor role. Free trade has not been the great job-killer — and neither has unchecked immigration, another of Mr Trump's favourite themes.

The United States admits about one million immigrants each year. Illegal immigration was once a major problem, but it has been reduced by nine-tenths over the past fifteen years. In 2015 the total was just one hundred and seventy thousand people, and it has since fallen further. Even counting the illegals, the United States receives only one new immigrant annually for every 282 people already in the country.

Canada, the country most similar to the United States in its economy and demography, admits three hundred thousand immigrants a year. Since its population is just over one-tenth of that of the United States, it is admitting immigrants at more than twice the American rate: one new immigrant annually for every 116 people already in the country. Yet there is no anti-immigrant outcry in Canada, no fear that the country is being overrun, and no labour-union opposition to the immigration policy. To the extent that American workers buy the idea that immigrants are depressing their wages or outright stealing their jobs, they are scapegoating the wrong people. It is the neo-liberal economic order (including free trade) that is depressing their wages, to be sure, but their job losses are due to one or the other of two radically different phenomena: computers, or the specific aspect of globalisation known as 'offshoring'.

Back in the late 1970s, when 'offshoring' began in a significant way, there was a direct substitution of foreign labour for American labour in industries such as textiles and furniture-making, and job losses were easily measurable. As the phenomenon gained speed through the 1980s and 1990s, there were still clearly identifiable cases where a factory shut down in the United States and re-opened again in Mexico or even China in order to exploit the far lower wages that prevailed in those developing countries. And in the grand old tradition of buccaneering capitalism, some masters of industry publicly flaunted their disdain for mere human considerations such as the jobs of fellow Americans.

> Ideally, you'd have every plant you own on a barge to move with currencies and changes in the economy.
> Jack Welch, CEO, General Electric, 1981–2001

But as we move forward through the 1990s, the picture gets muddier. Lots of IT jobs are being created abroad to serve American business (accountancy, billing services, call centres, and the like), but it is not clear that they would otherwise have become or remained jobs in the United States. Would those jobs have been done by Americans if there had been no foreign alternative, or would the companies just have invested in more automation because that would still be cheaper than paying Americans to do them? Some whole factories were still moving abroad, too, but once again there may have been a trade-off between more expensive automation at home and just moving the factory unchanged to a place with lower labour costs. What this means is that all estimates of how many jobs were 'lost' are inherently unreliable, but at a rough guess the United States lost a couple of million jobs to offshoring in the later 20th century out of a workforce (in 1979) of 104.6 million. Many more jobs have disappeared in the early 21st century, particularly in manufacturing, but few of them appear to have been exported.

In 1979 there were 19.6 million manufacturing jobs in the United States. Contrary to popular belief, that number only declined slightly in the next twenty years, remaining around 17.5 million right through the 1990s. Then it collapsed, and by 2009 (just after the financial crisis of 2008) it was down to 12.4 million. It dipped even further at the depth of the Great Recession in 2010–12, but had recovered to 12.4 million by 2017.[2] So something very big happened to American manufacturing in the first decade of this century, but it wasn't offshoring.

The key to this puzzle is the fact that American manufacturing jobs have declined by one-third in the past forty years, but American industrial production is now approximately twice what it was in 1979.[3] This can only be explained by much higher productivity per worker, and the presumption must be that the higher productivity is mostly due to automation, which transformed the way work was done in factories in the first decade of this century.

As Ball State University economics professor Michael Hicks observed in 2015, 'Had we kept 2000 levels of productivity and applied them to 2010 levels of production, we would have required 20.9 million manufacturing workers. Instead, we employed only 12.1 million.'[4]

That's where the jobs went, or most of them. Out of 7 million manufacturing jobs lost in the United States in the past forty years, at least 5 million were lost to automation. Then the manufacturers moved a lot of the remaining industrial jobs not abroad, but south and west to the 'Sun Belt', where unions are weak and the sun always shines, leaving behind the Rust Belt — which eventually gave us Donald Trump. The people whose incomes had been relentlessly squeezed for decades, and the people whose jobs had simply disappeared, finally struck back in 2016. Their aim wasn't very good, but their anger was entirely justified. They have been patient for a very long time.

Every time I drive through Detroit, it seems, they are tearing another skyscraper down: it's been empty for a decade or two (or three), the water has got in, bits are falling off, and they are dismantling it before it collapses into the street. That saddens me, because Detroit has the best Art Deco skyscrapers in the world, but I have no desire to engage in what is rightly condemned as 'ruin porn'. It's just a big city that has been having a hard time for a long time (as great cities sometimes do), but I choose it because it is a useful thread to lead us through the next part of the story: it is Motor City, the heartland of American manufacturing since the time of Henry Ford.

The initial downturn in Detroit's fortunes, after two generations of soaring prosperity — it still has one of the finest art galleries in America — was driven not by automation but by inequality: the injustices suffered by hundreds of thousands of African–Americans who had migrated north to work in the factories during the Second World War.

> People who have a stake in their society, protect that society, but when they don't have it, they unconsciously want to destroy it.
>
> Martin Luther King Jr.

The burning of much of Detroit's inner city in 1967 marked the beginning of a period of continuous decline that was steeper than in any other major American industrial city: Detroit's population has fallen by 60 per cent since 1950. Part of it was 'white flight' after the riots, and part was just a general drift to the suburbs; but from the mid-1970s on, wages ceased to keep up with rises in productivity for American workers, and from the early 1990s a great many jobs began to disappear in the automobile industry. Much the same was happening in other industrial cities, but the damage was most extreme in what was becoming known as the Rust Belt, and in 2016 the voters of that region delivered their verdict on the management of the American economy over the past generation. They elected Donald Trump.

No need to panic. If it's just a case of falling wages, that can be fixed, though Trump is probably not the person for the job. Wages can be tied to productivity again, income inequalities can shrink as well as expand, the anger can be soothed, and the system can be stabilised. It's what democratic politics does best, in fact. There's a kind of self-correcting feedback mechanism built into democracy: it operates over long time scales, which leaves a lot of room for ugly accidents, but it usually gets there in the end. Americans are beginning to digest the lessons of 2016, and it's likely that the platforms of the major parties will have taken account of the new political and economic realities by the next presidential elections in 2020. The anger level would then begin to go down — if it were not for the continuing rise of automation. Car-making was one of the first major industries to be remade by it, but automation is not finished with the Motor City.

For the past three generations, manufacturing vehicles has been the largest single industrial occupation on the planet. The global motor industry produced 95 million cars and commercial vehicles in 2016, up from 66 million only ten years before, and it directly or indirectly employed some 50 million people. If car-making were a country, it would have the world's sixth-biggest economy. And it's already pretty automated.

Assembly-line work was a prime target for early computer takeover, because it broke down the task of building a car, for example, into several hundred much simpler tasks that could each be done by a person who didn't require specialised skills. Some of the people on the assembly line were just attaching door handles and the like to each car as it trundled down the track, one on the left side and one on the right. Writing the program that would enable a robot arm to do that work instead was cheap and easy. Other jobs on the line required more skill, but with a little more investment you could write programs for them, too. In a few years the human population of that line dropped by 80 or 90 per cent — and most of the humans who remained were basically monitoring the machines doing the actual job. The same thing was also happening in all the other, smaller factories back up the supply chain where the headlight assemblies, the little electric motors, and all the other components that come together on the final assembly line were made.

Automation is an almost irresistible temptation for management because, from an employer's point of view, robots are much preferable to human workers, even if they cost the same or more. The robots don't take lunch breaks and toilet breaks, they'll work all day and all night, and they don't have to be paid overtime (indeed, they don't have to be paid at all), they don't demand sick leave or annual holidays, they don't join trade unions, and they don't sue you if they get mangled in some industrial accident. Not only that, but they are accurate, tireless workers (no more 'Monday morning cars'), and they generally do work out cheaper than humans in the end, despite their large up-front capital cost. What's not to love?

This wave of automation largely accounted for the huge fall in employment in manufacturing in the United States in the first decade of this century. Comparable numbers of new jobs were *not* created elsewhere, so the long-term unemployment rate went up permanently (although, as noted previously, much of this new unemployment was not regularly recorded). Even when people eventually did find new jobs, the number of months they spent without work while they were looking doubled in that decade. But then there was a lull.

The number of Americans working in manufacturing stabilised for most of the 'teen' years — and some of the factories that had been offshored in earlier years even began to be 'reshored' back to the United States, because so few people were now needed in the factories that it didn't matter all that much that American workers had to be paid more than Mexicans or Chinese. The convenience of having the production done at home, in a more predictable legal and political environment, outweighed the cost in higher wages. But the next round of job losses is about to begin. Let's stay with the car industry.

France and the United Kingdom recently announced that they will ban the sales of petrol- and diesel-engined cars from 2040. From then on, only zero-emission vehicles may be sold. India says it will institute a similar ban by 2030. China, the world's largest producer of cars — 28 million vehicles last year, more than the

United States, Japan, and Germany combined — is also planning to declare a ban soon, but is still working on the cut-off date. And the European Commission is planning to impose a minimum annual quota of electric vehicles (EVs) for all European car producers.

So if you were looking for a safe place for a long-term investment, you probably wouldn't choose the oil industry. Just over half of the 98 million barrels of oil produced in the world each day go directly to making petrol, used almost exclusively in motor vehicles. Another 15 per cent go to make 'distillate fuel oil', of which at least half is diesel fuel. So around 58 per cent of total world oil production is being used in vehicles now. There may be almost none in 35 years' time. Britain, for example, is planning to allow only zero-emission vehicles on the road (apart from a few specially licensed vintage cars) by 2050, only ten years after the ban on selling new cars with internal-combustion engines comes into effect. In practice, if these deadlines are observed, the cars on sale will be almost entirely EVs by the mid-2030s — and what's left of the oil industry will have a very different shape.

Countries that export most of their oil, such as Russia and Saudi Arabia, will find their incomes crashing for two reasons: sheer lack of demand, and very low prices ($40 per barrel or less) due to the huge glut of productive capacity. This may have major political consequences. Countries with some oil production of their own, such as the United States and China, will probably stop importing oil entirely. The US federal government will remain in the last ditch federally so long as Donald Trump is president — he's even trying to revive the coal industry — but eight states have already signed an agreement to have 3.5 million zero-emissions vehicles on the road by 2025. Millions of jobs will be lost in the oil industry as global production falls by at least half, although significant numbers of new jobs may be created in the renewable-power industries as electricity demand ramps up. But none of this has directly to do with computers and automation.

Some jobs will be lost in the car industry because electric vehicles are much simpler to manufacture, having many fewer moving parts than the old internal-combustion engines, but that's a small price to pay for the environmental benefits the EVs will bring with them. In any case, it's not really an automation issue, either. What will kill far more jobs, in the car factories and far beyond them, is the advent of self-driving cars, which most certainly is an automation issue.

Driverless vehicles will end up being ownerless vehicles. They will become public utilities, summoned when they are required for the specific trip you have in mind at the moment. Urban car clubs and peer-to-peer rentals are one precursor of this phenomenon; Uber and Lyft, in their different ways, are another.

Privately owned cars are parked an average of 95 per cent of the time. This figure varies little from one city or country to another, and illustrates why private car ownership will become a dispensable luxury. The difficulty in the past was gaining immediate access to a car for as long as you needed it at a reasonable cost unless you actually owned one, but the combination of the smart phone and the self-driving vehicle will solve that problem.

This, rather than a cheaper taxi service, is the real goal of Uber's business model, but once reliable self-driving cars are widely available, Uber will find itself deluged with competition. Private ownership will decline steeply: a recent KPMG survey of car-industry executives found that 59 per cent of CEOs believe that more than half of today's car-owners will no longer want to own a car by 2025.[5] In fact, there are hardly ever more than a quarter of privately owned cars being driven at the same time, so the total number of cars on the road worldwide may eventually crash to around one-quarter of the current number. That would eliminate most of the remaining jobs in the car-making industry.

The change goes wider than this, of course. Conventional buses and taxis will virtually disappear, taking millions of driving jobs with them. (There are a million taxi, Uber, and bus drivers in the United States alone.) Long-distance truckers and van drivers (another 3.5 million in the US) will also find work increasingly scarce: Daimler, Volvo, Uber, and Baidu are already road-testing the first self-driving 18-wheelers. And the changes still aren't finished.

About a quarter of the average central city in North America (less in Europe and Asia) is devoted to surface parking lots and multi-storey garages. They are part of the 95-per cent-parked problem. The car doesn't just take you downtown; it has to stay there the whole time you do, so it must be parked somewhere. Once people realise that most of this land is now available for redevelopment, it will get a lot easier and cheaper to live downtown: less commuting, more community. There may be quite a lot of new jobs in construction for a while as a result, but they won't be remotely comparable to the number being lost in the auto industry as a whole, and they won't last.

The same calculations for job losses apply elsewhere. Klaus Schwab, who runs the World Economic Forum (the annual shindig for the ultra-rich at Davos in Switzerland each January), illustrates the phenomenon vividly in his book *The Fourth Industrial Revolution*. (Never mind the 'Fourth' — it's just a conceit.) In 1990, Schwab points out, the three biggest companies in Detroit, all car-makers, had a market capitalisation of $36 billion, annual revenues of $250 billion, and 1.2 million employees. A quarter-century later, in 2014, the three biggest companies in Silicon Valley had a much higher market capitalisation ($1.09 trillion), earned approximately the same revenues ($247 billion), but only employed about one-tenth as many people (137,000).[6]

At different speeds and in different ways, this kind of thing is happening to a great many occupations, and the casualties will not be restricted to manual workers. Indeed, many manual jobs are quite safe at the moment: it will be a long time before we have autonomous robots capable of operating independently in the real world and doing forestry or fisheries work — or, for that matter, on-site plumbing and carpentry. Whereas white-collar jobs that require considerable education and intelligence but involve a lot of repetition, such as researching legal precedents or keeping medical records, are being rapidly eroded by automation right now. Take the case of Fukuoka Mutual Life Insurance, which is currently replacing the people who calculate its payments on insurance claims with an artificial intelligence (AI) system based on IBM's Watson Explorer.

It's a complicated job, reading medical histories and reports, checking certificates, calculating the length of hospital stays and the cost of surgical procedures, and spitting out the sum to be reimbursed to the client — and at Fukuoka Mutual it had to be done 132,000 times a year. That kept thirty-four employees busy in full-time jobs, but they were all laid off in March 2017, replaced by a computer system that cost $1.8 million to install but will save the company $1.2 million a year in wages.[7] If any job includes a lot of routine work, however complicated, it can be automated. If there are enough people doing that job to justify the expense of writing the software that will replace them, it *will* be automated eventually.

> Workers of the future will need to be highly adaptable and juggle three or more different roles at a time … There will be constant new areas of work people need to stay on top of.
>
> Anand Chopra-McGowan, head of enterprise new markets, General Assembly

The idea of continuous training is optimistic — I imagine there will be one-day training blitzes where people learn new skills quickly, and then are employed for a month when they're needed.

> Mark Spelman, co-head, Future of the Internet Initiative, member of the executive committee, World Economic Forum

We can't all be knowledge workers. So there will be a lot of unemployment — and perhaps no impetus to help these people. There will be a division between the few jobs that need humans, and those that can be automated.

> Dan Collier, CEO Elevate

Every day, somewhere on the planet, you will find a panel of academics, IT experts, and business people delivering 'wisdom' of this sort. In this case, it was a gathering called together by Deloitte UK, which provides 'audit, consulting, financial advisory and tax services', to ponder the Great Questions of the Day.[8] We've heard it all before, and our kids are already living in the 'gig' economy. The discussion needs to move on to questions such as, 'What kind of politics will we have with 50 per cent unemployment?' or 'Who's going to buy your products if you automate everybody out of a job?'

Actually, those are pretty easy questions. The answer to 'what kind of politics?' is that by then you will either have created a society that is serious about redistributing income in a way that we haven't seen for decades, or you will be living in a society that is on the brink of revolutionary violence (or has already fallen over the edge). And the answer to 'Who's going to buy your products?' is: nobody. People who have been automated out of their jobs have no money to spend on them. In the name of increasing efficiency and squeezing the maximum return out of your capital, you are destroying the consumer base on which a successful capitalism depends.

> The owner, the employees, and the buying public are all one and the same, and unless an industry can so manage itself as to keep wages high and prices low it destroys itself, for otherwise it limits the number of its customers. One's own employees ought to be one's own best customers.
>
> Henry Ford, 1926[9]

Ford practised what he preached: in 1914, he spontaneously doubled the wages of all his assembly-line workers to $5 a day and cut their work-day from nine hours to eight — and by the end of the decade, he had tripled his production of Model Ts to a million a year. But we aren't going to solve the coming Great Unemployment by such dramatic gestures. You can argue about how fast the change is going to come, debate which occupations will be hit first or hardest, quibble about each and every detail in the predictions, but the change will be huge and it is already on the way. Carl Benedikt Frey, one of the economists at Oxford University's Oxford Martin School whose analysis of which trades and professions were most vulnerable to automation in the United States was quoted in Chapter

One, is profoundly pessimistic about the rate at which jobs will vanish. (He and his colleague Michael Osborne saw 47 per cent of all American jobs as 'potentially automatable' in twenty years.)

'My reading of the evidence so far is that there will be less job-creating and ever greater labour-saving,' Frey said in a recent interview. 'If we look at the creation of new occupations by decades, they accounted for 8.2 per cent of new jobs in the 1980s, 4.4 per cent in the 1990s, and 0.5 per cent in the 2000s. It is not necessarily true that we will have a jobless future. But I struggle to use my imagination to see which industries will emerge to balance the loss of jobs.'[10] So we are probably looking at a future twenty years down the road that includes a very high rate of unemployment: not necessarily a 50 per cent jobless rate, for some new jobs will have been created, but almost certainly 35 or 40 per cent. We could be surprised by good luck and find that the problem turns out to be smaller than this, but it would be unwise to plan for that. Less than half such an unemployment rate gave us Donald Trump, so what can we do to avoid even worse outcomes in the future?

Well, consider what they did to avoid even worse future outcomes after the Second World War. The 1930s had ended extremely badly, and it was clear to most people that the rise of the fascist dictators had been greatly facilitated, if not actually caused, by the impoverishment of the working class and especially the lower middle class after the great stock-market crash of 1929. Unemployment rates in the major industrial countries surged to unheard-of levels — a peak of 25 per cent in the United States and 27 per cent in Canada in 1933, nearly 30 per cent in Germany in 1932 (just before Adolf Hitler came to power), and 29 per cent in Australia the same year — and radical politics of both the right and the left flourished almost everywhere. So once the Second World War was over, people in the democratic countries began to think about creating political and economic systems that weren't so vulnerable to popular rage. They created versions of the welfare state.

Most Western countries, both in Europe and overseas, already had old-age pensions, but the full set of state-provided services — from a comprehensive national health service free at the point of delivery, free education, and subsidised housing for the poor, to unemployment insurance, disability benefits, child benefits, and legal aid — were only instituted in most countries in the period 1945–1970. Even the United States developed a limited welfare state ('social security'), beginning with Franklin D. Roosevelt's New Deal in the 1930s, but it is significantly less ambitious than elsewhere — which may partly explain why popular anger is greater in the United States, and the political consequences more extreme. Of particular note is the fact that the United States is the only major developed country without a uniform and comprehensive national healthcare programme. Even if 'Obamacare' survives, some 25 million of the poorest Americans are still not covered, and most of the money passes through insurance companies rather than being administered directly by the government. As a result, American spending on health is the highest in the world — 17.6 per cent of Gross Domestic Product, compared to 11.4–12.0 per cent for France, Germany, the Netherlands, and Canada, and 9.1–9.6 per cent for the United Kingdom, Australia, New Zealand, Japan, Italy, and Spain — but health outcomes are roughly similar, regardless of spending.

It is not possible to say with confidence that the creation of more or less comprehensive welfare states was the key factor that kept Western politics off the radical road in the first half of the period since the Second World War, but it certainly helped to keep income inequality from getting out of hand. (It should also be recalled that during the Cold War the Western countries were competing with the communist-ruled states of Europe, all of which were full welfare states.) Equally, it cannot be proved that the switch to neo-liberal policies in the late 1970s, particularly in the 'Anglosphere', was enabled by the fact the lessons of the 1930s had been forgotten by then, but 40 years is a pretty plausible time-span for society-wide historical memory loss. At any rate, the forgetting was done, the income inequalities grew again, and here we are on Dover Beach with Donald Trump.

Compared to the people who built the welfare states 60–75 years ago, the political task that faces us now is not really that daunting. We aren't trying to rebuild after the biggest war ever, with half the cities of Europe and Asia bombed flat. We aren't all trapped in a new and potentially terminal global confrontation like the Cold War. We're very much richer than we were last time around. We just have to shrink the income inequalities that are radicalising our politics already, and come up with some solutions for the fact that a great many jobs are going to disappear no matter what we do, causing further destabilisation as they go. And, yes, it probably will involve expanding the welfare state further.

Within a couple of months of Trump's election, his canary-in-a-coalmine function had already produced its first and probably most important response: the revival of the old idea of a universal basic income (UBI). And its first high-profile outing, remarkably, was at the Davos meeting in January 2017, where several speakers were brought in to discuss the idea.

Well, not so remarkably perhaps, because the very rich are good at spotting emerging threats to their wealth and power, and the clear message of the US election was that the proles (and a lot of the old middle class) are angry and getting angrier. This will only get worse as automation advances, and at the same time the pool of potential customers for the goods and services whose sale keeps the whole capitalist economy afloat is shrinking as the jobs disappear. UBI is a tool that might cool the anger of people like Trump's supporters by shrinking the income gap, and at the same time put some purchasing power in their pockets. It is therefore gaining support on both the right and the left, and it is now part of any discussion of how social justice and political stability might be preserved in a democratic society where capital is replacing labour (for that is precisely what automation really does).

One cautionary note. Many of the proposals that are being made, and almost all of the pilot programmes that are being run in various countries at the moment, are about a basic income, but not a *universal* basic income. Typically, such basic incomes are just attempts to streamline the delivery of various state benefits such as unemployment payments, child benefits, rent subsidies, and the like into a single payment that is less encumbered with restrictions and conditions, cheaper to administer, and perhaps more generous. At best, these basic incomes are provided to the working poor as well as to the workless, and do not involve the usual docking of welfare payments as earned income rises, but they are payable only to people below a certain income level. President Richard Nixon's original 1969 proposal for a basic income for poor Americans was the first time such an idea reached the highest political level, but nowadays such proposals are commonplace.

A properly universal basic income, by contrast, goes to every citizen, rich or poor, as a matter of right with no strings attached. It should be enough to sustain a modest although not lavish lifestyle, and it does not decrease if the recipient is also in paid work. In the eyes of those who have recently fallen in love with the idea of UBI, the attraction is mainly that it may be able to prevent the social and political disaster that they fear automation will otherwise bring. It would not only keep the growing mass of people who have lost their jobs fed and clothed. Because *everybody* gets the universal basic income as a right, the argument goes, it would not stigmatise people in the same way that unemployment or welfare payments do. They would not feel humiliated by it, and so it would not breed the same misery, anger, and political extremism. And if the anger does not overflow, maybe democratic political systems can survive automation.

On the other hand, we should be aware that most people currently in the workforce, when asked to rank their preferences on a list that includes a higher minimum wage, laws that force firms to share some of their profits with employees, direct government subsidies to wages, and a universal basic income, will put UBI in last place. This may be mostly just that they are more comfortable with the familiar options, but it may also be because they are very reluctant to break the link between work and compensation. It makes the shift from being economically necessary to being surplus to economic requirements too open and too obvious. One sympathises, but if the jobs are really going to vanish, such preferences will have to give way to reality. And if the subsistence farmers of two centuries ago could make the transition to urban workers in industry and commerce who were paid in cash, today's urban workforce can probably make a gradual transition to a more leisured existence without suffering a collective nervous breakdown.

We are probably in the early stage of a global economic transformation comparable to the industrial revolution, when entire populations went from being overwhelmingly rural to overwhelmingly urban in only two generations. This time, the transformation is from a full-employment economy to an economy of abundance that only requires a fraction of the population to work. But that does not necessarily or even probably mean a division of society into two castes, one of which does all the work while the other lazes around. It's much more likely to be a society where most people work part-time or drop in and out of work for periods of months or years, although there will obviously be some at the extremes who work all of the time or none of it.

The industrial revolution was an angry, turbulent time, with urban uprisings and class warfare. We'll be lucky if the damage this time is limited to demagogues like Donald Trump, who pander to the fear and anger of the newly displaced — and not just the displaced of the old working class, but the growing numbers of middle-class people who are also being displaced by machines. They are not 'right wing' in the traditional sense, although many have become more socially conservative, and some openly racist, as their panic rises. 'Populist' is a much better word: they hate the changes and the 'elites' who seem untouched by them, and they want their old jobs and their self-respect back. But the old jobs are not coming back, and even populist politics cannot resurrect them.

Besides, many of these people actually hated their jobs, from which they were only free for two weeks (in the US and Japan) or at most five weeks (in Europe) a year. The real task will be to find ways to provide a growing minority of our fellow citizens with money and self-respect without those jobs. They may become the majority in the end, just as UBI may be the answer in the end, but in the meantime it will have to be the old patches: higher minimum wages, stronger trade unions, perhaps a legal linkage between productivity gains and wage rises, and unemployment and welfare payments that do not automatically shrink or vanish when the recipient finds some low-paid casual work (some form of basic income, perhaps, though not the universal kind).

What we are going through now is not a disaster; it's a process. Last time, it took over a century of mass misery and occasional mass bloodshed to get through it, but at the end most people were living much longer, healthier, more interesting lives than their peasant ancestors. We should try to do it a lot better and quicker this time.

7

Growing Pains

Five minutes later and it wouldn't have mattered so much. It was a quite shocking cock-up … The mice were furious.

Douglas Adams, *The Hitch-Hiker's Guide to the Galaxy*

The mice were 'protrusions into our dimension of hyper-intelligent beings' who had commissioned the construction of Earth as the site for a big and long-running experiment that involved a semi-intelligent species called human beings, for obscure purposes known only to themselves. They were furious because five minutes before the experiment was due to end and deliver its results, the Earth was demolished by Vogon contractors to make way for an interstellar bypass.

Adams's masterwork is one of the funniest and cleverest books of the 20th century, but the point (as he well knew) is that the Earth is indeed the site of a big and long-running experiment involving human beings. It's called civilisation, and its purposes, if any, are obscure. But we are all caught up in this experiment, and its outcome certainly matters to us and to the biosphere we now dominate. To understand where that experiment is now, and where we might choose to take it next, we need a narrative (though not one with hyper-intelligent mice in it).

Narratives are important. The world does not come with a script, and narratives are the main way that human beings reduce the daily avalanche of political, social, and economic events to a manageable story. They are never completely accurate, mainly because they have to omit so much of the detail, but they are indispensable — and they are the most valuable service (or disservice) that journalists and historians can provide. Here, in a rather large nutshell, is the narrative of this book. It is about how human beings order their societies, and in particular about the idea of equality.

The obsession with equality is the primary social distinction between *homo sapiens* and the other great apes, and it derives pretty clearly from our superior reasoning and language abilities. Only human beings (and perhaps others of our immediate lineage, such as the Neanderthals and the Denisovans) could have reached the subtle but immensely important conclusion that 'All men seek to rule, but if they cannot rule they prefer to remain equal' — and then acted on that insight in the first great rebellion. The revolt of the underdogs probably dates back to the time when language became complex enough to allow a 'large, well-united coalition of subordinates' to 'deny political power to the would-be alphas in their group,' but we do not know when that was. Probably not much more than a hundred thousand years ago, because if human beings had been capable of such complex coordination during the previous inter-glacial warm period (130,000–115,000 years ago), it's likely that the agricultural revolution and the rise of civilisations would have happened then. (They certainly didn't waste any time when the next inter-glacial warm period began around eleven thousand years ago.)

The rebellion that overthrew the alphas had to be repeated ten thousand times in ten thousand scattered bands to produce the hunter-gatherer world of universal, vigorously enforced egalitarianism between adult males that existed before the rise of civilisation. (Gender equality was not part of the original package, but it is the logical and irresistible extension of it.) The revolution may have spread quickly once the first successful examples of an egalitarian society emerged, so it's quite possible that this state of grace lasted as much as 50,000–100,000 years, long enough (2,000–4,000 generations) for some genetic changes reinforcing the human preference for equality to occur. Or maybe there have been no such changes. Maybe any social species with a strong dominance drive and the intelligence to see that unless such a drive is curbed, it will leave the losers in the race (that is, almost everybody) in a subordinate position, would have taken the same action to enforce equality. We don't have to choose between these possibilities. All we need to know is that strict equality between adult males is a human tradition of long standing. The dominance drive was not removed, but it was thoroughly suppressed.

And then at the end of the last major glaciation came the rise of agriculture and a very rapid growth in the total human population. The average size of human groups rose even more steeply, and by five thousand years ago there were already a number of early civilisations that included hundreds of thousands of human beings. By now, the alphas had already escaped from their long containment and taken over: all of these civilisations were tyrannies, because they could not be run any other way. No doubt some early mass societies tried to preserve the egalitarian principle, but in the new conditions they could not successfully compete with more efficient, centrally directed tyrannies. The egalitarian societies must have been winnowed rapidly and ruthlessly, because they survive only in foundation myths of a lost Golden Age.

For the great majority of human beings, the rise of civilisation was a disaster. Not only did they lose their independence, being reduced from free men and women to slaves and serfs, but they were worse off in material terms. Their diet, mostly grain, was so poor in nutrition that the average height of adults in the early civilisations was at least 10 per cent below that of hunter-gatherers. They suffered from many epidemic diseases that had not troubled their ancestors, because the disease vectors easily transferred from their domesticated animals, most of which lived in herds and flocks, to human hosts who now also lived in herd-like conditions. Their numbers went up, but their average lifespans probably went down, and they were certainly having much less fun.

All this went on for a very long time, and there

were only two consolations. One was that the toll of lives exacted by war went down. Among the hunter-gatherers, every man was a warrior, everybody lived on the front line, and inter-band warfare was virtually constant; in civilised societies, warfare was sporadic and was generally waged by a specialised class of soldiers. The other consolation, almost invisible at the time, was that gradually (but very, very slowly) knowledge was accumulating in a way that it could not have done before the invention of writing. The rate at which it accumulated was also accelerating, though that too was so slow as to be almost imperceptible.

The principle that human beings are fundamentally equal in status vanished utterly from the material world for all of this time — yet it remained alive in the new religions of the 'axial age', and also in the non-hierarchical friendship circles, of about the same size as a small hunter-gatherer group, that almost everybody in the mass societies created for themselves. Encoded in our genes, or just remembered in our dreams, equality continued to have a strong hold on our imaginations — and eventually, nine or ten thousand years after the first unwitting pioneers drifted into part-time farming, the accumulation of knowledge finally achieved critical mass and exploded into the modern world.

By the 14th–16th centuries CE, the global population had risen to around half a billion, most of them concentrated in four major Old World civilisations. The Indian civilisation was in the course of being conquered by Muslim invaders, however, while the heartlands of the Islamic civilisation had been severely damaged by the Mongol invasions. China's technological innovations — such as the printing press, paper, gunpowder, the magnetic compass, and ocean-going ships —were more impressive than Europe's, but it proved less adept at putting them into practical use than the Europeans.[1] There was also an intellectual revolution underway in Renaissance Europe that ultimately resulted in the adoption of the scientific method, which gave Europe a big technological, industrial, commercial, and military lead over the rest of the world. It was therefore the Europeans who colonised three of the six inhabited continents, largely supplanting the indigenous inhabitants of North America, South America, and Australia, and who ultimately conquered most of Africa and Asia as well.

It could have been just another replay of the tawdry old tale of imperial expansion, followed eventually by imperial retreat and collapse — indeed, that scenario did play out again, in the end — but there was something else going on at the same time. What Europeans called the Enlightenment was a broad shift in values and sensibilities that elevated reason above faith, and advanced the ideas of liberty, tolerance, and 'fraternity' (for which read 'equality') — and the printing press, cheap paper, and mass literacy allowed these ideas to spread through entire populations. The first democratic revolutions happened in the late 18th century in countries with mainly European populations, precisely and solely because of the early European lead in adopting the one potential mass medium of the time, the press.

There was little in pre-Renaissance European history to suggest that Europeans cared more about equality than did Arabs, Indians, or Chinese. The West was actually resurrecting values that were the common political heritage of all human beings, but the people of these countries came to believe that human rights, equality, and democracy were exclusively Western cultural values. (Nevertheless, the principle that everybody is equal eventually destroyed the European overseas empires, because it turned out that the non-European subject peoples demanded it, too.)

The industrial revolution got underway at about the same time, and it was one hell of a ride. Between 1750 and 2010 the human population increased tenfold, and the proportion of the world's land area devoted to raising food and therefore withdrawn from natural systems increased from 7 per cent to 40 per cent.[2] Over the same period, the Sixth Mass Extinction got underway, and the amount of carbon dioxide in the atmosphere increased from 280 parts per million to 400 ppm. Wars continued as before, but with far more destructive weapons: the Second World War killed at least 40 million people, and by the end nuclear weapons were dropped on cities. None of this should be seen as surprising or particularly wicked: the industrial and scientific revolutions put the human species on a very steep learning curve, and there was bound to be a lag between the new realities and our comprehension of them.

The multiple environmental and technological threats that face us today were implicit in the pattern of our development from the start, and there is no sense in flagellating ourselves about it. Any other intelligent species that suddenly gained mastery over its environment would probably have behaved in much the same way, and would face the same threats at this point in its career. A population explosion was inevitable. The over-exploitation and degradation of natural systems long before we realised the implications of what we were doing was inevitable. Tribalism, death camps, and nuclear weapons were inevitable.

But we didn't do all that badly, given where we started from. In less than three hundred years, we have virtually eradicated the ancient institutions of slavery and serfdom, ended all the traditional empires, and made a start on gender equality. We have even abolished the death penalty in most countries, and torture is illegal everywhere (though in practice it survives in many countries). In 1750, there were no democracies in the world; now almost every country gives at least lip service to the principle that everybody has equal rights and value. About half the world's population lives in countries that are formally democratic, although all democracies fall short of their ideals, some by a very long way. Wars continue, but no great powers have fought each other directly since 1945. (They used to fight each other all the time, and it was perfectly legal to start a war whenever you felt like it.) There are even global organisations such as the United Nations and the International Court of Justice that try to create a system of international law which bans aggression and protects human rights. It's all very much a work in progress, but the progress has been significant. We are a long way down the road from where we started, although there is still a long distance to cover.

We are a young species on the make, and we are in the midst of a vast, millennia-long experiment called civilisation that we never actually signed up for. It may succeed if we can adapt our traditional attitudes and behaviours to our new circumstances. That means mutual respect, global cooperation, limited intervention in natural systems, and a democratic political culture that puts a high value on equality and restraint — all the things that the cynics sneer at. Alternatively, we may fail to adapt and thereby bring our civilisation down around our ears, either in a single orgy of destruction (for example, worldwide nuclear war and nuclear winter, or truly runaway climate change), or in an extended series of lesser calamities — military, political, and environmental — that destroy most or all of the major centres of civilisation.

The survival of the human race is not at stake. As James Lovelock, the creator of the Gaia hypothesis and the leading contemporary contender for Charles Darwin's crown, once said to me, 'Human beings are tough. A few breeding pairs will always survive.' A much-diminished human race would presumably just go back to the old ways that served us well for more than 100,000 years. (There would be little chance for a 'second-generation' industrial civilisation to arise later on, because we have used up the easily accessible sources of fossil fuels the first time around.) Lots of other species would become extinct, but mass extinctions are just business as usual: the only unusual aspect this time is that the agent driving it is a single dominant species. The biosphere has gone through mass extinctions much more destructive than the one that is currently getting underway, and within one or two million years the survivors diversified into a plethora of new species that filled all the available ecological niches.

But that is only one of a range of possible outcomes. There could be much better ones if we have the time and the political will to stop the damage we are doing to vital natural systems before it undermines our ability to sustain the current global civilisation. How much time we have is unknowable, but a serious and concerted global effort to restore the self-regulating systems that used to maintain a stable environment would probably still stand a fair chance of success. As for the will, don't look to dictators to provide it. They have to devote most of their energy to staying in power, and have little left over to devote to larger issues. Totalitarian political systems are particularly bad in this respect, even when their declared goal is equality. There have been few environmental and ecological disasters as extreme as the Soviet Union after seventy years of communist rule, or China today.

There were some extremely destructive attempts to achieve complete equality in the 20th century. The communist experiment, drawing more on Rousseau than on anthropological evidence — 'man is born free, but is everywhere in chains' — set out to recreate an idealised world of equality, possessions held in common, and no state. It discovered, after some tens of millions of deaths, that complete equality could only be obtained in a world of varying individual abilities and many material possessions by rigidly enforced political, social, and economic controls on everything and everybody — and even then the enforcers were more equal than the others. The conclusion that was drawn from that long nightmare was that a certain degree of inequality must be tolerated in an industrialised mass society in order that liberty and general prosperity may flourish. But we have never agreed on how much inequality is tolerable.

The political will required to deal successfully with great issues such as war and environmental destruction is far more likely to be available if most countries can hang on to their democracies, retain the rule of law at home, and continue to expand it in the international domain as well. The current outbreak of angry populism is a threat to all that, but it is actually about equality. The anger is growing because inequality has become too great, because too many people feel they have been left behind and forgotten. It could even be seen as a kind of regulating mechanism whose function is to keep democratic political systems with capitalist economies from toppling into hugely unequal oligarchies.

A populist backlash that goes unanswered may end up creating an authoritarian regime — a 'fascist' regime, in the common parlance. Generally nationalist and often racist, these regimes claim to defend the interests of those who have been betrayed and victimised (the Common People or the 'left-behinds'), and demand absolute power in return. The ideology is usually pretty rudimentary, but there are almost always villainous foreigners and treacherous domestic ethnic or religious minorities who must be kept down or out, or in extreme cases simply destroyed. A number of such regimes have appeared recently in fledgling democracies with shaky economies — such as Sisi's Egypt, Erdoğan's Turkey, and Duterte's Philippines — but there are no Western democracies that are currently fascist or even near it. Nevertheless, many people in the West fear that the current of events is flowing in that direction.

It does feel like a current at the moment, but it may actually be more like a pendulum. There was huge unemployment in the Great Depression of the 1930s, the inequalities became intolerable, and several fascist states did emerge in developed countries as a result. They caused a terrible war, but after they were defeated the pendulum swung the other way for thirty years: the democracies spent the period 1945–1975 building welfare states, in large part to stop the inequalities from widening again. They had learned their lesson.

And then, of course, they forgot it again (the same old story of generational turnover erasing societal memory), and inequalities multiplied unchecked for more than four decades. The existence of the welfare states slowed the build-up of resentment the losers felt as they fell further and further behind, but eventually it boiled over. And so we come to the present day and the election of Donald J. Trump. As a wake-up call, it's a lot less terrifying than the Second World War, and it may even have come in time.

> There is a line among the fragments of the Greek poet
> Archilochus which says: 'The fox knows many things,
> but the hedgehog knows one big thing.'
>
> Sir Isaiah Berlin, *The Fox and the Hedgehog*, 1953

Apart from his role as the canary in the coalmine, how
does Donald Trump fit into the narrative of human
history that I have sketched above? He has only a bit
part, really. Trump is an inconsequential person who
discovered one very important political fact — that there
is a large reservoir in the United States of angry people
who feel that they have been cheated of their birthright
of good jobs and left to rot by the neo-liberal economy
— and he has exploited that fact to boost himself into
the presidency. But that is the only big thing he knows.
He doesn't know how to rescue those angry people from
their plight, or even seem very interested in trying. He
is only a messenger, and after delivering his message he
might as well leave.

He won't do that, of course. He still seems to be
enjoying the ride, although at some point he might
tire of it and simply resign. But Trump is essentially
purposeless. His two major political goals, as measured
by the volume of his tweets, are the repeal of the
Affordable Care Act ('Obamacare') and the abrogation of
the Joint Comprehensive Plan of Action (the multilateral
agreement that stops any Iranian work on nuclear
weapons for the next ten years.) But he is curiously ill-
informed on both issues, as he was also about the Paris
climate agreement that he has already withdrawn from.
(He talked about 're-negotiating' it, when it was not

negotiated in the first place. Each country simply made a voluntary offer to cut its greenhouse-gas emissions by an amount it determined for itself, and the sum of those promises was the agreement.) What really seems to motivate Trump in all three cases is just a desire to destroy Barack Obama's political legacy, for reasons known only to himself.

In every case, he can hope for at best only partial success. The Republican majority in Congress is so divided on what should replace the Affordable Care Act that it has so far proved incapable even of repealing it. And all one hundred and ninety-three other signatories of the Paris climate accord have stated that they will fulfil their commitments, despite the defection of the United States. Other countries are already used to making international treaties that the US either refuses to ratify or subsequently withdraws from because of the vagaries of American domestic politics. They just carry on regardless, on the assumption that the US will eventually catch up when the political situation at home is more favourable.

In the particular case of the climate-change agreement, probably the most important of the deals at risk, the damage done by the American withdrawal may turn out to be slight or even non-existent. The US is responsible for 14 per cent of global greenhouse-gas emissions, but Trump's decision to withdraw from the accord cannot legally take effect until November 2020 (when he might be seeking re-election, but might even have already withdrawn from the race.) Moreover, many American cities and states have pledged to maintain or expand their planned cuts in emissions, despite the failure of the federal government.

Donald Trump's antics are endlessly fascinating to the media, and to some extent he has even colonised our minds — despite my best efforts, I find it hard to get through a day without a conversation with somebody about his overnight tweets — but his actual influence on events is turning out to be surprisingly small. The United States is very little different today from what it was when Trump first entered the White House, and his impact on American affairs may ultimately rank with that of Warren G. Harding and Millard Fillmore. This is not so surprising, really, as his great success in life has been not as a 'deal-maker', but as a TV host and entertainer. Besides, it is hard to get much done when you have a really short attention span. The only way Trump could have a large impact on history is by stumbling into a war somewhere.

Well, no, there is one other impact. Without his election victory in November 2016, it might have been many years more before we really awoke to the fact that democratic political systems are losing support among large minorities of our own populations. Fixing that problem will be a task that spans a generation, but at least we now know what the job is — and we even have some notion of where the solutions (partial and temporary, as always) might lie.

Before I ran for President, I read a book called *With Liberty and Dividends for All: how to save our middle class when jobs don't pay enough*, by Peter Barnes, which explored the idea of creating a new fund that would use revenue from shared national resources to pay a dividend to every citizen, much like how the Alaska Permanent Fund distributes the state's oil royalties every year … Once you capitalize the fund, you can provide every American with a modest basic income every year … I was fascinated by this idea, as was my husband, and we spent weeks working with our policy team to see if it could be viable enough to include in my campaign. We would call it 'Alaska for America.' Unfortunately, we couldn't make the numbers work … We decided it was exciting but not realistic, and left it on the shelf. That was the responsible decision. I wonder now whether we should have thrown caution to the wind and embraced 'Alaska for America' as a long-term goal and figured out the details later.

Hillary Clinton, *What Happened*, Simon and Schuster, 2017, p. 239

Yes, she should have, although she might have lost the election anyway. Universal Basic Income was still an unfamiliar idea for most ordinary Americans at the time, and few people in the 'lower 48' states even knew what the Alaska Permanent Fund is. It is a state-owned investment fund that was created from the Alaskan government's oil revenues, and it pays out a dividend each year to every man, woman, and child living in Alaska. The dividend goes up and down depending on how the investments are performing and what the oil price is, but in recent years the cheques that are sent out have varied from $800 to $2,000 per person (that is, $8,000 for a family of four). It is a real Universal Basic Income, though not one big enough to sustain a person who has no other income, and half a million Americans in Alaska, rugged individualists though they all undoubtedly are, seem to be very happy with it.

Could such an arrangement work at the national level? Why not? It might be of benefit in every country in the world, but it certainly looks like a promising solution for all the developed countries. The wealth is there: the United States has lost 7 million industrial jobs since 1980, but industrial production has more than doubled in the same time: the robots are doing a great job. It's just a question of finding an acceptable way of distributing the wealth more equally. Given the scale of the damage that automation is probably going to do to the job market in the relatively near future, finding such a way is an urgent political priority, not just in the United States but in every developed economy.

The objections to UBI come in two quite distinct categories: fiscal, and what you might call moral. The sums of money required to pay everybody in the society enough money to live on are clearly very large, and opponents of the concept have a field day calculating how much income tax would have to go up to cover it. John Rentoul, chief political correspondent of *The Independent*, recently estimated that the standard British tax rates of 20, 40, and 45 per cent would have to go up to 48, 68, and 73 per cent to pay for a universal basic income of £8,320 ($US11,290) a year.[3] But this is nonsense: nobody is proposing to finance UBI solely or even mostly out of income taxes. Much of the cost would be met simply by funnelling the government money that is currently spent on state benefits that would no longer be needed — from unemployment and welfare payments to old-age pensions — into the UBI system.

Let's take the province of Ontario as an example. It has set the basic income for its pilot project at CAD$1,400 per month, on the calculation that this is the minimum amount needed to provide an acceptable (though not lavish) standard of living. That's CAD$16,800 per person per year, although it would obviously have to be more for people living in very expensive places like Toronto and for many people living with disabilities. There would be other exceptions, too: the monthly payment for couples living under the same roof might be less than twice the individual amount, and there would have to be extra money for people with dependent children. But bureaucracies exist precisely to deal with that sort of complications. For now, let's stay with the basic figure.

Multiply $16,800 by the number of people aged eighteen and over who would receive it if there were a nationwide Universal Basic Income (29 million in Canada's case), and the annual bill for UBI in Canada would come to about $487 billion a year. The Canadian federal budget in 2017 projected government spending of $330 billion, and the ten provinces together spend about another $320 billion: total $650 billion. One-third of that amount is currently 'social spending',[4] so say $200 billion a year nationwide on old-age pensions, unemployment insurance, child benefits, welfare payments and the like. All of these programmes would be replaced by a universal basic income, and the money that was formerly spent on them would be funnelled into the UBI instead. That would cover about 40 percent – two-fifths – of the cost of a national UBI paid at the rate of the current Ontario pilot programme. Where would the rest come from?

Some would come from income taxes, but not necessarily by raising them. If everybody, rich or poor, has an additional $16,800 of annual income, it will boost a large number of people into a higher tax bracket for the last proportion of their income. They would nevertheless wind up with more income than before (but they'd still complain anyway). That extra tax revenue would still leave a gap in the funding, but more creative solutions can be imagined.

> Certainly there will be taxes that relate to automation. Right now, the human worker who does, say, $50,000 worth of work in a factory, that income is taxed and you get income tax, social security tax, all those things. If a robot comes in to do the same thing, you'd think that we'd tax the robot at a similar level … I don't think the robot companies are going to be outraged that there might be a tax. It's OK.
>
> Bill Gates, February 2017[5]

Gates, like other leading Silicon Valley figures (Facebook co-founders Mark Zuckerberg and Chris Hughes; SpaceX co-founder and CEO of Tesla Inc. Elon Musk; and eBay founder Pierre Omidyar), believes that the spread of automation and artificial intelligence will make the adoption of a Universal Basic Income inevitable, and they are taking a personal interest in it. The one UBI pilot in the United States is in California, but it's not being funded by the state government. Instead it's being financed by the moguls of Silicon Valley, maybe as penance for having created the automation that caused the problem in the first place — or maybe just to avoid being strung up from a lamp-post when the revolution comes.[6] If the alternative to UBI is a generation of people living on welfare because automation has destroyed their jobs, and a level of anger and political alienation that threatens to destroy democracy, ways will be found to fund it.

The second practical question is: would a Universal Basic Income destroy people's will to get up in the morning and go out to work? It's an important question, because even if automation does kill 47 per cent of existing jobs in the next twenty years, this means that 53 per cent of them will still need to be done by human beings. Finding an answer to this question is the main purpose of the various experiments with UBI that are now underway, but there is some encouraging evidence from the few places where it has already been tried. There is no detectable decline in the willingness to work of Alaskans who get their cheques from the Permanent Fund Dividend each year — and inequality among Alaskans fell in the 1990s and 2000s, while it increased in every other American state.[7]

There is considerably stronger evidence from Iran, which has been providing a universal basic income to its citizens for the past eight years. When former president

Mahmoud Ahmadinejad cut bread and energy subsidies in late 2010, he replaced them with a cash payment for all Iranians that amounted to 29 per cent of the median household income, free of all strings — a genuine and quite substantial Universal Basic Income. Indeed, it initially amounted to 6.5 per cent of Iran's Gross Domestic Product. Its value has subsequently been eroded by high inflation (which was mainly due to the tightening of international sanctions on Iran in 2011, but was widely blamed on the UBI by the middle class). These cash payments have had a major impact in terms of reducing income inequalities in Iran, and a recent research paper found that they did not lead to a fall in the average hours worked or in the likelihood that recipients would be employed, even in the poorest sections of the population. There were many press reports that workers were abandoning their jobs and farmers leaving their farms because of this modest increase in their incomes, and the Iranian middle class, as convinced as any other middle class that the poor are just lazy, mostly believes these reports, but the researchers found no evidence for these allegations.[8]

And then there is intriguing evidence from the past: historical data from an experiment in the Canadian province of Manitoba in 1974–79, known at the time as Mincome (minimum income). Sponsored jointly by the Manitoba government and the Canadian federal government under prime minister Pierre Elliott Trudeau, it conducted a randomised controlled trial in the city of Winnipeg and in one rural town, Dauphin, in which groups of lower-income families were given sums ranging from CAD$3,800 to $5,480 a year ($16,000–$24,000 in today's money). The research focussed on whether such payments would be a disincentive to work for the recipients, but the results were skewed by the fact that it was not an unconditionally guaranteed income: payments were reduced by 35 per cent, 50 per cent, or even 75 per cent for every dollar they earned by working. As in some similar experiments in New Jersey, Seattle and Denver when the Nixon administration was considering introducing a guaranteed income for all poor Americans, working or not, in the early 1970s, the Mincome research revealed that the impact of the basic income on employment choices was minimal: family size, the availability of jobs, and other extraneous factors had a much bigger effect on whether the men and women in the study were working or not. There were some interesting non-employment effects, though: later studies showed that the basic income caused less social stigma than conventional welfare, that more teenagers finished school because they were under less pressure to support their families, that new mothers stayed at home longer with their babies, and that hospital visits dropped by 8.5 per cent. (In Canada, they also found that the divorce rate went up, as women suddenly had the financial independence to leave bad and abusive relationships.)[9]

And that's it: all the data we have on how UBI might affect willingness to work. It's quite positive, as far as it goes, but much further research is needed. And much is being done: in addition to the American and Canadian pilot programmes, there are others underway or scheduled in the Netherlands, Finland, Italy and Scotland. At the other end of the wealth scale, a universal basic income scheme in Kenya, launched by a New York-based non-profit called GiveDirectly, has started giving ninety-five people in a village in western Kenya the less-than-princely sum of $22.50 a month each. It almost doubles their cash income, they are free to save or spend it as they see fit, and the payments will last for twelve years. The charity plans to expand the programme to some two hundred villages eventually, and to monitor the decisions people make over the full twelve years.[10]

Most of these early experiments with a guaranteed income are aimed only at poor people, or even only at *unemployed* poor people, and the stated measure of success is generally how many of them get back into paid work. Meanwhile, however, the researchers will be gathering valuable data about the actual behaviour of people who have a guaranteed basic income, so that when the supporters of UBI come back with concrete proposals for national systems in five or ten years' time, they may have much more solid arguments than they do now.

Finally, the *moral* objection to UBI, if that's the right word, is that people deprived of work will suffer from existential angst because all meaning and purpose will have vanished from their lives. Without work, they will suffer a paralysing identity crisis and find it impossible to fill their days, and having to rely on a UBI will only make matters worse. Their sense of meaninglessness can only be cured by jobs – even if we have to invent them. There are a number of possible responses to this, some of which are polite enough to be printable.

In 2015, the YouGov polling organisation conducted a quite serious poll in the United Kingdom about the meaning of work. It was triggered by a rash of anonymous signs that had greeted London commuters one day earlier that year saying things like, 'It's as if someone were out there making up pointless jobs for the sake of keeping us all working,' and 'Huge swathes of people spend their days performing tasks they secretly believe do not really need to be performed.' The poll revealed that 37 per cent of working British adults already believed their job was not making a meaningful contribution to the world. Only 50 per cent thought that it was, and the rest were unsure. (In terms of their trades and professions, by the way, those who felt pointless were more likely to be consultants, bankers, lawyers, accountants, etc. than care workers, teachers, or bus drivers.) So there's one quite large part of the population who are definitely not relying on their work to give meaning to their lives. And here's another clue: a different YouGov poll in the previous year found that 57 per cent of British people supported the introduction of a four-day work week.[11]

You can take this attitude to extremes, of course. There is an irreducible minority of people — maybe 5 per cent, maybe less — who will choose to sit around and drink beer all day (or the female equivalent, which my wife suggests is watching daytime television). They would certainly do it under any imaginable form of UBI because they are already doing it now, living off welfare payments or their spouses or boy/girlfriends. UBI would let them do it more comfortably, but it is doubtful that it would substantially increase their number. Nevertheless, the thought that they would get away with it enrages many people. There is a very strong popular belief that people should work for a living, even if the society as a whole is very rich and the work doesn't actually need to be done, and this prejudice applies especially strongly to the poor. As Harvard economist John Kenneth Galbraith once put it, 'Leisure is very good for the rich, quite good for Harvard professors — and very bad for the poor. The wealthier you are, the more you are thought to be entitled to leisure. For anyone on welfare, leisure is a bad thing.'[12]

There's not much you can do about people who hold this prejudice except to wait for them to age out of the population, but the fretting about what people will do when they no longer have paid work is greatly overdone. A large minority of the adult population in every country is not working already — some because there are no jobs for them, others because they are the parents of small children, or disabled, or too rich, or retired, or just lazy and feckless. For the most part, they find ways to pass their time to their own satisfaction (if they have any spare time). Some do voluntary work, some travel, some drink beer or smoke dope while watching Netflix, some write unpublished novels, and some tinker with their cars or tend their gardens, but we are not currently faced with a crisis of mass anomie. There are undoubtedly workaholics who would suffer greatly if deprived of work, but such people are probably a small minority of the population.

At a guess, there are just as many people today who hate the jobs they are compelled to do by harsh economic necessity as there would be people who would hate their lack of paid work in an automated future where they were sustained economically by UBI. Most people would probably be fine, particularly if UBI took the shame and humiliation out of not having a job. There are the inevitable predictions about a not-too-distant future when the robots have taken all the jobs and human beings spend all their time playing enhanced virtual-reality games, of course, but we'll cross those bridges if and when we get to them. For the moment, at least, we can file these predictions in the same bin as the 'Singularity', when the AI takes over and humanity becomes redundant. In the real, flesh-and-blood future of the next two or three decades, the task will be to keep democracy from being overwhelmed by the speed and scale of change – and there is a little understood side-effect of UBI that could be very helpful in this regard. By reducing income inequality quite radically, it would also reduce almost all the social ills that might otherwise overwhelm a society where many or most of the jobs have suddenly vanished.

[A]mong the richest countries, it's the more unequal ones that do worse according to almost every quality of life indicator ... per capita GDP is much less significant for a country's life expectancy, crime levels, literacy and health than the size of the gap between the richest and poorest in the population.

David Cameron, *The Guardian*, Hugo Young Lecture, 10 November 2009

Cameron was still six months away from the UK election that made him prime minister when he delivered that lecture for *The Guardian*, but he was clearly reading up on the things he would need to know if he won the job — and the one book that a 'One Nation' Conservative politician like him needed to read in 2009 was *The Spirit Level: why equality is better for everyone.* The authors, Richard Wilkinson and Kate Pickett, two epidemiologists with a flair for statistics (a necessity in that trade), had set out by trying to explain the big differences in life expectancy — the 'health inequalities' — between people at different levels in the social hierarchy. As they wrote in their preface, 'the focal problem initially was to understand why health gets worse at every step down the social ladder, so that the poor are less healthy than those in the middle, who in turn are less healthy than those further up.'[13]

In the United States, the answer might be 'because the poor cannot afford good medical care', but Britain, like most rich countries, has a free National Health Service available to all. Yet life expectancy in the United Kingdom is barely a year longer than in the United States. The one common factor that seems to drag them both down to the bottom of the life-expectancy table for rich countries is the fact that they both have a very high degree of income inequality by comparison with most other developed countries. It makes no difference how high a given country's per capita income is: Japan's is around $10,000 per person less than the US, but the Japanese live on average four years longer than Americans. (The Japanese have the lowest level of income inequality of any developed country.) It doesn't matter how much they spend on healthcare, either: the US spends half again as much per person as the United Kingdom, but Americans still die younger. (Income inequality in Britain is not quite as great as it is in the US.) The only measure that matters, it seems, is how big the income gap is between the rich and the poor *inside* any given country.

'Hmm. I didn't expect that', said Pickett to Wilkinson. (Or maybe he said it to her. I'm imagining this conversation, but it must have happened quite early in their research.) 'I wonder what else lines up with income inequality.' And suddenly what had been up to that point a fairly standard piece of epidemiological research turned into a wide-ranging investigation of the global impact of inequality. They looked at rates of mental illness and drug use in 23 rich countries: both correlated very closely with the degree of income inequality. They looked at the rate of obesity and the teenage birth rate: same thing. They looked at educational performance and the violent crime rate: same again. They looked at the rate of imprisonment and the lack of social mobility: everything lined up with the degree of income inequality, to an uncanny extent. And when they looked at the plight of the United States, the country among the 23 studied with the greatest difference between the incomes of the top 20 per cent and the bottom 20 per cent, and with the worst outcomes on most health and social issues, they were emboldened to say:

> The relationships between inequality and the prevalence of health and social problems ... suggest that if the United States was to reduce its income inequality to something like the average of the four most equal of the rich countries (Japan, Norway, Sweden and Finland) ... rates of mental illness and obesity might each be cut by almost two-thirds, teenage birth rates could be more than halved, prison populations might be reduced by 75 percent, and people could live longer while working the equivalent of two months less per year.[14]

The 'income' in these calculations and comparisons is not relevant as a measure of the resources available for health care. All the countries that Wilkinson and Pickett studied are rich enough that adequate resources for health care should not be a problem. Instead, the differences in income serve as a rough-and-ready indicator of the distance between the various social classes — and it is that distance that makes all the difference. The negative social and health outcomes in societies with major income inequalities, they conclude, are mainly driven by the frustration and resentment that individuals feel at being embedded in what amount to dominance hierarchies: the very thing we have been trying to escape from for the better part of forever. And it is not only the poor who suffer: all but the very rich have worse health outcomes in societies with highly unequal incomes.[15]

There has been a good deal of further research done on this topic since *The Spirit Level* was first published in 2009, and most of it confirms Wilkinson's and Pickett's observations.[16] We have quite suddenly come into possession of a powerful new tool: we now know that most of the social and health problems that we try to treat separately are closely linked to one single economic fact that it is within our power to change. Reducing income inequality radically will not abolish crime or mental illness or addiction or heart disease, but it *will* make them all far less common.[17] The egalitarian hunter-gatherer who still dwells within us all will not be so stressed, so frustrated, so angry, and so we will treat ourselves and others a lot better. The relationship really is that simple and that direct.

My focus in this book has not been on social and health issues, unless they directly affect the stability and survivability of the democratic political order, but I cannot resist pointing out that if we should adopt a universal basic income to protect ourselves from a job apocalypse and runaway populism, it would have the added benefit of healing many of the social wounds opened up by great disparities in income. A UBI that made almost no difference to the income of the highly paid and had only a modest effect on middle-class incomes would almost double the income of the lowest-paid. If you want to shrink the income inequality in society, nothing could have a bigger and faster impact than UBI.

We are all prone to a degree of self-dramatisation, but we are not living through a great crisis of democracy. It's a rather small crisis, with so far not too many hurt: growing pains, not a terminal illness There have been bigger crises in the past, and there will probably be bigger crises in the future. But this is our crisis, and we do have to get through it.

The rise of Donald Trump is forcing us to analyse the problems that brought him to power: inequality, exacerbated by automation. The world, and particularly the developed countries, will waste a couple of decades in futile political infighting if we don't deal with those issues successfully, at a point in our history when climate change is looming and we can't afford to waste time.

We certainly don't have time for wholesale changes in our economic system, because that sort of thing uses up all the available political energy for decades: if you want to overthrow capitalism, leave it for later. What we need now is a quick fix that reduces inequality to a tolerable level and restabilises our democracies. If UBI is not the right answer, we need some other solution that ticks the same two boxes: ensuring that everybody has a decent income despite the unstoppable advance of automation, and doing it in a way that does not humiliate those who no longer have jobs.

It's not rocket science. If we can't solve this problem, we really don't deserve to get any farther.

Acknowledgements

My thanks to my sons, Owen and Evan, and my friends Peter Neary and Harry Tucker for reading the manuscript and offering their very helpful comments. And to my wife, Tina Viljoen, for that and a great deal more.

Notes

Chapter One: A giant orange canary

1   'Immigrant Population by State, 1990–Present', Migration Policy Institute, <www.migrationpolicy.org/programs/data-hub/us-immigration-trends>.

2   Federica Cocco, 'Most US manufacturing jobs lost to technology, not trade', *Financial Times*, 2 December 2016.

3   Sarah O'Brien, 'That shiny new car is out of reach for many Americans', *CNBC*, 28 June 2017, <www.cnbc.com/2017/06/28/that-shiny-new-car-is-out-of-reach-for-many-americans.html>.

4   Nicholas Eberstadt, *Men Without Work*, Templeton Press, West Conshohocken, PA, 2016, p. 22.

5   Dulguun Batbold and Ronald A. Wirtz, 'Disability and Work: challenge of incentives', *fedgazette* (Federal Reserve Bank of Minneapolis), 29 January 2015.

6   Christina Beatty, Steve Fothergill, and Tony Gore, 'The Real Level of Unemployment 2017', CRESR, Sheffield Hallam University, October 2017.

7   'Automation and Independent Work in a Digital Economy', *OECD Policy Brief,* May 2016, <www.oecd.org/employment/future-of-work.htm>.

8   'Technology at Work v2.0: the future is not what it used to be', Citi GPS: Global Perspectives & Solutions, January 2016.

9   Richard Berriman and John Hawksworth, 'Will robots steal our jobs? The potential impact of automation on the UK and

other major economies', *UK Economic Outlook*, March 2017, <www.pwc.co.uk/economicservices/ukeo/pwcukeo-section-4-automation-march-2017-v2.pdf>.

10   Nico Jaspers, 'What do Europeans think about basic income?', *BIEN*, 22 May 2016, <http://www.basicincome.org/wp-content/uploads/2016/05/EU_Basic-Income-Poll_Results.pdf>.

Chapter Two: Don't touch that button!

1   Yochi Dreazen, 'Candidate Trump promised to stay out of foreign wars. President Trump is escalating them', *Vox*, 25 August 2017, <https://www.vox.com/world/2017/8/25/16185936/trump-america-first-afghanistan-war-troops-iraq-generals>.

2   Piers Morgan, 'Donald Trump on sex, money and politics', *GQ Magazine*, 7 August 2015, <http://www.gq-magazine.co.uk/article/gq-entertainment-donald-trump-interview-piers-morgan>.

3   'Texts of Accounts by Lucas and Considine on Interviews With MacArthur in 1954', *New York Times*, 9 April 1964.

4   Bernard Brodie, ed., *The Absolute Weapon: atomic power and world order*, New York, Harcourt Brace, 1946, p. 76.

5   '"A rogue" and a 'dotard': Kim Jong-un's statement on Trump in full', *The Guardian*, 22 September 2017, <https://www.theguardian.com/world/2017/sep/22/a-rogue-and-a-gangster-kim-jong-uns-statement-on-trump-in-full>.

6   Samantha Raphelson, 'Lawmakers Fear President Trump's Authority To Launch Nuclear Weapons', *Here and Now* (National Public Radio), 17 November 2017.

7   Shane Harris and Matthew M. Aid, 'Exclusive: CIA files prove America helped Saddam as he gassed Iran', *Foreign Policy*, 26 August 2013, <http://foreignpolicy.com/2013/08/26/exclusive-cia-files-prove-america-helped-saddam-as-he-gassed-iran/>.

8   Graham Allison, 'Is Iran still Israel's top threat?', *The Atlantic*, 8 March 2016, <https://www.theatlantic.com/international/archive/2016/03/iran-nuclear-deal-israel/472767/>.

9   Kim Sengupta, 'Donald Trump is "greatest threat to international security", says former MI6 head', *The Independent*, 23 June 2017, <http://www.independent.co.uk/

news/world/middle-east/donald-trump-greatest-threat-international-security-mi6-sir-john-sawers-herzliya-israel-security-a7805251.html>.

Chapter Three: The EU and Brexit

1   Nick Hopkins and Rowena Mason, 'Exclusive: what Theresa May really thinks about Brexit shown in leaked recording', *The Guardian*, 26 October 2016, <https://www.theguardian.com/politics/2016/oct/25/exclusive-leaked-recording-shows-what-theresa-may-really-thinks-about-brexit>.

2   YouGov Survey Results, EU Referendum Vote, 23–24 June 2016.

3   See Chapter Five, pp. 112–3.

4   The correct adjective is murine, not rodentine, but sometimes clarity is better than accuracy.

5   Frans de Waal, 'Do Humans Alone "Feel Your Pain"?', *The Chronicle of Higher Education,* 26 October 2001.

6   Charlene Rohr, Alexandra Pollitt, David Howarth, Hui Lu, and Jonathan Grant, *What Sort of Brexit Do the British People Want? A Proof-of-Concept Study Using Stated Preference Discrete Choice Experiments,* Rand Europe Publications, 13 July 2017.

7   'Poorer than their Parents? Flat or Falling Incomes in Advanced Economies', *McKinsey Global Institute,* July 2016.

Chapter Four: Democracy

1   Peter Davison, ed., *George Orwell: a life in letters,* London, Liveright, 2011.

2   Harold K. Schneider, *Livestock and Equality in East Africa: the economic bases for social structure,* Bloomington, Indiana University Press, 1979, p. 210.

3   Christopher Boehm, *Hierarchy in the Forest: the evolution of egalitarian behavior,* Cambridge, Harvard University Press, 1999, Kindle Locations 2119–20.

4   Bruce Knauft, 'Violence and Sociality in Human Evolution', *Current Anthropology*, 1991, Vol. 32, pp. 391–428.

5   Boehm, 'Egalitarian Behavior and Reverse Dominance Hierarchy', *Current Anthropology,* 1993, Vol. 34, pp. 227–54.

6   Mellon Foundation Symposium on Egalitarian Behavior, Dept.
         of Anthropology, Emory University, Atlanta, 1995.

7   Boehm, *Hierarchy*, Kindle Locations 915–29.

8   The entire quote, from 'Say that a man …' is from Boehm,
         Hierarchy (Kindle Locations 648–68), but the informant's
         remarks (indented) are taken from Richard B. Lee, *The !Kung
         San: men, women and work in a foraging society*, Cambridge,
         Cambridge University Press, 1979.

9   Donald Alexander Mackenzie, *Indian Myth and Legend*,
         Glasgow, Gresham, 2014, p. 107.

10   Thomas Merton, *The Way of Chuang Tzu*, New York, New
         Directions, 1969, p. 76.

Chapter Five: Trump

1   Brian Schaffner and Stephen Ansolabehere, *Cooperative
         Congressional Election Study 2016*, published August 2017.
         (Ansolabehere, Stephen; Schaffner, Brian F., 2017, 'CCES
         Common Content, 2016', doi:10.7910/DVN/GDF6Z0, Harvard
         Dataverse, V3, UNF:6:Hacct7qJt1WXOGPb63A5Gg==; CCES
         Guide 2016.pd).

2   Stephen Clarke and Dan Tomlinson, *In the Swing of Things:
         what does Donald Trump's victory tell us about America?*,
         Resolution Foundation, 18 November 2016.

3   Ed Pilkington, 'Trump v the media: did his tactics mortally
         wound the fourth estate?', *The Guardian*, 23 November 2016.

4   Moonves was speaking at the Morgan Stanley Technology,
         Media & Telecom Conference in San Francisco. Paul Bond,
         'Leslie Moonves on Donald Trump: "It May Not Be Good for
         America, but It's Damn Good for CBS"', *Hollywood Reporter*,
         29 February 2016.

5   Emily Stewart, 'Donald Trump Rode $5 Billion in Free Media
         to the White House', *The Street*, 17 November 2016, <https://
         www.thestreet.com/story/13896916/1/donald-trump-rode-5-
         billion-in-free-media-to-the-white-house.html>.

6   David Leonhardt and Kevin Quealy, 'The American middle
         class is no longer the world's richest', *The New York Times*,
         22 April 2014.

7   Thomas Palley, *Financial Crisis to Stagnation: the destruction
         of shared prosperity and the role of economics*, Cambridge,

Cambridge University Press, 2012, p. 147.

8   *State Motor Vehicle Registrations, by Years, 1900–1995*, Federal Highway Administration, April 1997, <https://www.fhwa.dot.gov/ohim/summary95/mv200.pdf>.

9   Larry Elliott, 'Governments have to invest in the fourth industrial revolution', *The Guardian*, 17 July 2017.

10   Josh Bivens, Elise Gould, Lawrence Mishel and Heidi Schierholz, 'Raising America's Pay: why it's our central economic policy challenge', Economic Policy Institute, Briefing Paper #378, 4 June 2014.

11   Bivens et. al., ibid.

12   *The Guardian,* 8 November 2011.

13   John Seip and Dee Wood Harper, *The Trickle-Down Delusion: how Republican upward redistribution of economic and political power undermines our economy, democracy, institutions and health — and a liberal response,* University Press of America, 2016, p. 161. Has the United States finally reached peak title?

14   US Bureau of Economic Analysis, 'US Real GDP Growth Rate by Year', Multpl, <www.multpl.com/us-real-gdp-growth-rate/table/by-year>.

15   Seip and Harper, ibid., p. 166.

16   Dani Rodrik, *The Globalization Paradox: why global markets, states, and democracy can't co-exist*, OUP, p. 75.

17   Ben Smith, 'Obama on small-town Pa.: clinging to religion, guns, xenophobia', *Politico*, 11 April 2008, <http://www.politico.com/blogs/ben-smith/2008/04/obama-on-small-town-pa-clinging-to-religion-guns-xenophobia-007737>.

18   Katie Reilly, 'Read Hillary Clinton's "basket of deplorables" remarks about Donald Trump supporters', *Time*, 10 September 2016.

19   Zachary Newkirk, 'Donald Trump's donations to Democrats, Club for Growth's busy day and more in capital eye opener: February 17', *OpenSecrets Blog*, 17 February 2011, <http://www.opensecrets.org/news/2011/02/donald-trumps-donations-to-democrats/>.

20   Janell Ross, 'Obama revives his "cling to guns or religion" analysis — for Donald Trump supporters', *Washington Post*, 21 December 2015.

21   Wade Wilson, 'Trump's election is going to be the biggest fuck you ever recorded in human history', 10 November 2016, <https://www.youtube.com/watch?v=nlKiYV47NBw>.

22   George W. Bush, 'National Security and Homeland Security Presidential Directive' NSPD 51/HSPD-20, <https://fas.org/irp/offdocs/nspd/nspd-51.htm>.

23   Jonathan Freedland, 'Welcome to the Age of Trump', *The Guardian*, 19 May 2016.

Chapter Six: Globalisation or automation

1   'Trade in Goods and Services 2016', *OECD Data*, 2017, <https://data.oecd.org/trade/trade-in-goods-and-services.htm>.

2   Drew Desilver, 'Most Americans unaware that as US manufacturing jobs have disappeared, output has grown', Pew Research Centre, 25 July 2017.

3   Ibid.

4   Michael J. Hicks, *The Myth and the Reality of Manufacturing in America*, Ball State University Center for Business and Economic Research, June 2015, p. 4.

5   Patrick McGee, 'Carmakers face threat from new drivers of profit', *Financial Times*, 8 August 2017.

6   Klaus Schwab, *The Fourth Industrial Revolution*, London, Penguin Random House, p. 10, Kindle Location 229.

7   Justin McCurry, 'Japanese company replaces office workers with artificial intelligence', *The Guardian*, 6 January 2017.

8   Printed as part of *The Guardian Roundtable*, 13 October 2016.

9   Jeff Nilsson, 'Why Did Henry Ford Double His Minimum Wage?', *Saturday Evening Post*, 3 January 2014.

10   Tim Adams, 'My father had one job in his life, I've had six in mine, my kids will have six at the same time', *The Observer*, 29 November 2015.

Chapter Seven: Growing pains

1   Jared Diamond's brilliant book *Guns, Germs and Steel* offers a plausible explanation. He suggests that China's geography (a smooth coastline with few deep indentations, no impassable mountain barriers in the interior, and big rivers for long-distance transport) facilitated its unification under one ruler,

whose whims could shut down whole areas of commercial and technological development. Thus, for example, China's fleet of giant ocean-going junks ('treasure ships'), which explored the Indian Ocean and the East African coast under the command of Admiral Zheng He, were decommissioned in the 1430s when the Confucian faction at the imperial court gained ascendancy over the eunuch faction, and all sea-going vessels were ordered to be destroyed by the Jiajing emperor in 1525.

By contrast, Europe consists of many big peninsulas, and is carved up by many mountain ranges. For that reason it was never successfully unified under a single ruler: there were always dozens of separate states, which meant that an innovator whose idea was rejected by one government could shop it around to others until somebody bought it. Thus the Genoese Cristoforo Colombo, when he couldn't convince the Portuguese king, the governments of the republics of Genoa and Venice, or King Henry VII of England that the world was small enough that one could sail straight west to Asia, simply went and sold that (mistaken) notion to the Spanish monarchs Ferdinand and Isabella instead. His ships were a quarter the size of Zheng He's treasure ships, but they discovered the Americas and triggered the European conquest of most of the world.

2   The actual dates for the latter statistic are 1700–2005. James Owen, 'Farming Claims Almost Half Earth's Land, New Maps Show', *National Geographic News*, 9 December 2005

3   *The Independent*, 2 January 2017.

4   Statistics Canada, 'Government spending on social services', *The Daily*, 22 June 2007, <https://www.statcan.gc.ca/daily-quotidien/070622/dq070622b-eng.htm>.

5   Kevin J. Delaney, 'The robot that takes your job should pay taxes, says Bill Gates', *Quartz*, 17 February 2017, <https://qz.com/911968/bill-gates-the-robot-that-takes-your-job-should-pay-taxes/>.

6   The tech start-up incubator Y Combinator, which runs the Silicon Valley project, has announced that it will conduct the experiment in two as yet unnamed states. Three thousand people representing a variety of demographics and income

levels will receive a fixed income — in the best cases, $1,000 a month — for up to five years with no strings attached. Ryan Brown, 'Silicon Valley giant Y Combinator to give people varied amounts of cash in latest basic income trial', *CNBC*, 21 September 2017, <https://www.cnbc.com/2017/09/21/silicon-valley-giant-y-combinator-to-branch-out-basic-income-trial.html>.

7   Tyler Prochazka, 'Prestigious British think tank endorses basic income', *Basic Income News*, 19 December 2015, <http://basicincome.org/news/2015/12/united-kingdom-prestigious-british-think-tank-endorses-basic-income/>.

8   Djavad Salehi-Isfahani and Mohammad H. Mostafavi-Dehzooei, 'Cash Transfers and Labor Supply: evidence from a large-scale program in Iran', Working Paper 1090, *Economic Research Forum*, May 2017, <http://erf.org.eg/wp-content/uploads/2017/05/1090.pdf>.

9   Gregory Mason, 'Revisiting Manitoba's basic-income experiment', *Winnipeg Free Press*, 23 January 2017; 'Mincome', *Wikipedia*, 20 October 2017, <https://en.wikipedia.org/wiki/Mincome>.

10   Austin Douillard, 'US/Kenya: new study published on results of basic income pilot in Kenya', *Basic Income News*, 27 March 2017, <http://basicincome.org/news/2017/03/us-kenya-new-study-published-results-basic-income-pilot-kenya/>.

11   Will Dahlgreen, '37% of British workers think their jobs are meaningless', *YouGov UK*, 12 August 2015, <https://yougov.co.uk/news/2015/08/12/british-jobs-meaningless/>.

12   Elizabeth Mehren, Interview with John Kenneth Galbraith, *Los Angeles Times*, 12 December 1999.

13   Richard Wilkinson and Kate Pickett, *The Spirit Level: why equality is better for everyone*, London, Penguin, 2010, p. ix.

14   *Ibid.*, p. 168.
15   *Ibid.*, pp. 176–77.
16   *Ibid.*, pp. 190–91.
17   *Ibid.*, pp. 18–24.

Index

absolute equality, 99–100
    destructive aspects, 174–5
Access Hollywood tape, 121
Adams, Douglas, 165
adult literacy *See* literacy rates
Affordable Care Act (US), 159, 177
    See also Obamacare
Africa *See* Kenyan UBI programme;
    !Kung social controls; San
    bushman hunter-gatherers; South
    Africa
African National Congress, 85–6
Age of Perfect Virtue (China), 102
agricultural revolution, 168
    impact on egalitarianism, 100–1,
    103
Ahmadinejad, Mahmoud, 49, 185
Alaska Permanent Fund, 180–1
    effect on willingness to work,
    184
Alliance of Liberals and Democrats
    for Europe, 74
alpha types
    dominance of, 168
    suppression of, 89, 94, 166–7
al-Sisi, General, 7, 176
Alternativ für Deutschland (AfD),
    4, 55, 56
American politics, difference from
    European politics, 4–5
American Revolution, 7, 28

American War of Independence
    1776, 106
Andropov, Yuri, 83
The Art of the Deal (Trump, 1987),
    114
artificial intelligence (AI), impact on
    white-collar jobs, 154
Australia
    health spending, 160
    immigration in, 77
    unemployment rates in 1920s
    and 1930s, 159
automation
    impact on jobs, 17–18, 181
    impact on manufacturing
    industry, 10–11, 145
    impact on motor industry, 147–9
    impact on service industries, 11
    impact on white-collar jobs,
    153–4
    jobs at risk of, 17–18
    percentage of jobs at risk, 156–7
    See also self-driving cars; self-
    driving trucks
axial age, 169
    mass religions, 27
Ayatollah Khomeini, 46, 49

Baidu, 152
ballistic missiles *See* intercontinental
    ballistic missiles (ICBMs)